MW00791811

ONE TAKEN

A Lawyer's Guide to Being Sure You Are a Christian

Brett Preston

RIVER BIRCH PRESS

Daphne, Alabama

One Taken by Brett Preston
© 2021 Brett Preston
All rights reserved. This book is protected under the copyright laws of the United States of America. This book may not be copied or reprinted for commercial gain or profit.

Scripture quotations marked CSB have been taken from the Christian Standard Bible ®, Copyright © 2017 by Holman Bible Publishers. Used by permission. Christian Standard Bible ® and CSB ® are federally registered trademarks of Holman Bible Publishers.

Scripture quotations marked NIV are taken from the Holy Bible, New International Version®, NIV®. Copyright © 1973, 1978, 1984, 2011 by Biblica, Inc.™ Used by permission of Zondervan. All rights reserved worldwide. www.zondervan.com, The "NIV" and "New International Version" are trademarks registered in the United States Patent and Trademark Office by Biblica, Inc.™

Scripture quotations marked NRSV are from New Revised Standard Version Bible, copyright © 1989 National Council of the Churches of Christ in the United States of America. Used by permission. All rights reserved worldwide.

ISBN 978-1-951561-84-0 (print)
ISBN 978-1-95156?-85-7 (e-book)
For Worldwide Distribution
Printed in the U.S.A.

River Birch Press
P.O. Box 868, Daphne, AL 36526

"That is how it will be at the coming of the Son of Man. Two men will be in the field; one will be taken and the other left. Two women will be grinding with a hand mill; one will be taken and the other left. Therefore keep watch, because you do not know on what day your Lord will come" (Matthew 24:39-42 NIV).

"I tell you, on that night there will be two in one bed; one will be taken and the other left. There will be two women grinding meal together; one will be taken and the other left" (Luke 17:34-35 NRSV).

Test yourselves to see if you are in the faith. Examine yourselves. Or do you yourselves not recognize that Jesus Christ is in you?— unless you fail the test (2 Corinthians 13:5 CSB).

All Scripture is inspired by God and is profitable for teaching, for rebuking, for correcting, for training in righteousness, so that the man of God may be complete, equipped for every good work (2 Timothy 3:16-17 CSB).

Contents

Introduction

Are you are a Christian? Are you sure? If not, it sounds like you need a lawyer. Wait, what? A lawyer, not a member of the clergy? Yes, a lawyer—at least to start the process of becoming sure you are a Christian. We have work to do before you go to the clergy. Here's why.

Let's say life hands you a difficult situation. There's a massive amount of information to consider, and you don't even know where to start. You can make sense of some of it, but it's hard to figure out what is relevant. Important information is scattered all over the place. Plus, you know there are rules you have to follow, but you can't begin to identify them all, much less be sure you are following them.

A lawyer can help. Lawyers are very good at bringing order to chaos. When given a task and a massive amount of disorganized information, lawyers identify the parts that are relevant and extract them. Then they organize the relevant information in a way that makes each piece, and its relationships to other pieces, easy to understand. They also figure out what rules apply and how to follow them.

Lawyers bring order to chaos to help their clients answer hard questions, solve problems, make informed decisions, and follow rules. All of these things are much easier to do when the client has the benefit of the well-organized, relevant information the lawyer assembled and the solid understanding of the rules the lawyer helped the client acquire.

Now let's come back to your desire to be sure you are a Christian. You may be one of the many people who believe they are Christians but still have doubts about their faith. You may wonder whether you can really be a Christian because you engage in certain behaviors or hold certain beliefs. You may also have doubts because you have struggled with reading the Bible, so you don't have the information you need to be sure.

That is understandable. The Bible is poorly organized from the perspective of a person who wants to get a good command of everything it says about a given subject; in that respect, it is chaotic. Some people never read the Bible because they find it impenetrable. Others try to read it, searching for the answers to their questions, but give up, frustrated at how hard it is to find what they are looking for. Perhaps you are one of those people.

Again, it sounds like you need a lawyer. If you have doubts about your faith because you are unfamiliar with the Scriptures and are concerned that your behavior is incompatible with being a Christian, a lawyer would be well suited to help you.

- *You have a hard question:* How can you be sure you are a Christian?
- *You have a problem:* The verses that hold the answer to that question are like needles in a biblical haystack.
- *You need to make an informed decision:* How to conduct yourself as a Christian.
- *You need to know rules:* The rules that apply to you as a Christian.

If you asked me to use my skills as a lawyer to help you answer this hard question, solve this problem, make this decision in an informed way, and understand the rules, I would approach that task the same way I would handle any other client's matter. I would:

- Read the massive amount of disorganized information in the New Testament;
- Identify all of the verses that are relevant to how you become a Christian, how you can be sure that you are, and the rules Christians are supposed to follow;
- Organize those verses by subject; and
- Deliver them to you, along with my limited commentary, in a form that is easy for you to understand and use.

In other words, I would write this book. I am a Christian, but I didn't write this book as a Christian. I wrote it as a lawyer helping a client. That client just happened to be me. I had the same questions and problems you do, and addressed them by doing for myself what I said I would do for you. I then turned my work into this book after realizing that readers like you might benefit from my efforts.

Before you consult a member of the clergy, my part of the work was to provide you, in a user-friendly arrangement, all the verses you need to read. That's done. Your part is to read them. When you have, you will be able to assess your status as a Christian with confidence. You will either (i) not have any doubts about your standing as a Christian or, if you do, (ii) be able to articulate exactly what the doubts are and why you have them, with reference to specific verses in the Scriptures. You can then discuss your specific doubts with your preferred priest or pastor, who will be able to give you specific guidance. The importance of going through this process is obvious. You have only one opportunity to get this right, and it is easy to get it wrong.

Rich and Mandy had dated for years. They got along famously, wore out the words "I love you," and stayed together through some difficult times. Rich realized Mandy was the one. He bought a ring and invited her to dinner, not telling Mandy that he also invited friends and family, who were secluded when the host sat them at their candlelit table. On cue, they surrounded Rich and Mandy, phones recording, when he got down on one knee and asked her to marry him.

Mandy said no. She loved Rich, but, for purposes of marriage, he wasn't her type. Rich was confused and devastated. How could two people experience the same relationship but have such different understandings of its true nature? How could he not have known she was going to reject him?

The same thing may be happening with you and God. You could be spending your life sincerely believing that you and God have one relationship when in fact you have another. He loves you dearly, but may not be ready to marry you because, not actually being a Christian, you are not his type. You don't want to find this out when God gives you the bad news in front of everyone who has ever lived, and after it's too late to do anything about it. You need to be sure you and God have the same understanding of your relationship, and you need to be sure now. This book can help with that.

Finally, given the way things are these days, I have to come out and say this: I did not write this book to help you pass judgment on whether someone else is a Christian. I wrote it to help you determine whether you are a Christian. In other words, I hope these pages will allow you to be certain that, whether in the Rapture or after you die, you will be one taken.

Preface

ORGANIZATION

Comparing how the Bible and *One Taken* are organized makes it easy to see the value this book brings to people who want to be sure they are Christians. Both books contain the verses you need to read to have confidence you are a Christian. Finding those verses in the Bible is like going on an Easter egg hunt. Finding them in this book is like someone handing you a basket of already-found Easter eggs.

THE BIBLE

The Bible is in two parts, The Old Testament and The New Testament. The Old Testament contains 39 writings, each of which is commonly referred to as a "book." All books in the Old Testament were written many years before Jesus lived. I did not include Old Testament verses in this book because the New Testament tells you everything you need to know to become a Christian and be sure that you have done so.

The New Testament contains 27 writings, also called "books," all of which were written in the decades following Jesus' death. There is some debate about who actually wrote a number of the books of the New Testament. The short story is that it's complicated. Since that issue is complicated and doesn't really matter for purposes of this book, I will regard each book as having been written by the person the Bible says wrote it and leave it to you to explore this interesting (but here irrelevant) question.

The first four books are called the Gospels of Matthew, Mark, Luke, and John, which are accounts of Jesus' life and teachings. The next book, Acts, is Luke's historical account of the early days of the Christian church, which sprung up in the months and years after Jesus was crucified, rose from the dead, and ascended into heaven. The rest of the books of the New Testament, except the last, are actually letters. The apostle Paul wrote most of them, others a few, some to early churches and others to individuals. The last book, Revelation, is John's prophecy about things that will happen leading up to and including Jesus' return in the Rapture, and then the aftermath.

Given the Bible's diverse topics, authors, and arrangement, it should come as no surprise that the verses you need to read to be sure you are a Christian are scattered throughout the New Testament. Finding them can be daunting.

ONE TAKEN

In contrast, *One Taken* makes it easy to find the relevant verses: it puts them all in one place at one time for you. Each chapter opens with a brief discussion of the topic it addresses and then, section by section, quotes all of the verses in the New Testament on that topic. It includes just enough commentary to help you process the verses you are reading and see the relationships of each topic to the next. What could be easier?

I considered putting the verses in order based on their significance, but reasonable people may disagree about the relative significance of particular verses. Also, all verses are significant in their own way. I decided to keep the verses in the order they appear in the New Testament. That way, if you are following along in your Bible to read the verses in context (which you might consider doing), you can just turn pages from the start of the New Testament to the end as you go from verse to verse, rather than jump around.

In light of the significance many people place on verses that quote Jesus directly, I put those verses under "Jesus" subheadings. Verses that contain his disciples' teachings, but do not directly quote Jesus, appear under the "Disciples" subheadings.

You will see that I quoted verses from three different but excellent translations of the Bible: the New International Version (NIV); the New Revised Standard Version (NRSV); and the Christian Standard Bible (CSB). They are my preferred translations; you may prefer another one. You may also find that different translations suggest different meanings of a particular verse that is of importance to you. I encourage you to explore those differences and any significance they may have to your faith. I did not do so here, however, in favor of keeping my eye on the ball: efficiently delivering to you the verses you need to read to have confidence that you are a Christian.

I tried to keep my own commentary about what the Bible says to a minimum. My goal was to say enough to help you work your way through the verses without paying the price of hearing me go on and on about them. I hope I struck that balance to your satisfaction.

There are rooms full of books and articles written on the issues this book addresses; you will have no trouble finding additional information. Before you turn elsewhere for input, however, I suggest that you assess your status as a Christian based on the verses in this book. You are perfectly capable of reading the verses, understanding them, and evaluating where you stand in light of them. What others may have to say is of secondary importance.

Having said that, the Bible contains verses that are inconsistent with one another. Sorry, that's just the way it is. Plenty of commentators have opinions about how to reconcile them; their opinions are just a few internet searches away. You may want to include them among the sources and authorities you consult to broaden your understanding of the Bible after you get a good command of what it actually says by reading this book. You will probably find that their opinions also differ, leaving you much where you started.

So how do you resolve issues about which there are inconsistent verses? You may not be able to. That's where faith comes in: faith that God loves you and has your best interests at heart, and that all that is unclear will become clear someday. In the meantime, get yourself squared away with respect to the issues about which the Bible offers perfect clarity.

Perhaps the most important point about the verses quoted in this book is this: This is what they say. Are they politically incorrect by today's standards? Some are. Do they set a standard that is difficult to meet? Yes. In fact, if you are like most people, even most Christians, you will probably find that at least some of your behavior does not even come close to measuring up to the standards they set. But none of that changes what they say.

If some of your behavior or beliefs do not measure up, does that mean you are not a Christian? Only you can answer that question. I hope this book will help you do so.

PART I

ARE YOU A CHRISTIAN?

The first things you have to do to be sure you are a Christian are (i) understand what it takes to become one, and (ii) determine whether you have done those things.

This part of the book inventories and organizes the verses that explain what you have to do and how each of those things plays a role in making you a Christian.

1

We Are Sinners

Before we get to what it means to be a Christian, we should first consider why it even matters if you are. It matters because we are sinners, and without Christ, our sins will leave us eternally separated from God.

Philosophers have debated for years whether people are good or bad by nature. No one would suggest, however, that anyone (except Jesus) has ever lived their entire life without doing something wrong, or sinning. Even Paul, who wrote most of the books of the New Testament, recognized and struggled with his own sinful nature:

> For I know that good itself does not dwell in me, that is, in my sinful nature. For I have the desire to do what is good, but I cannot carry it out. For I do not do the good I want to do, but the evil I do not want to do—this I keep on doing. Now if I do what I do not want to do, it is no longer I who do it, but it is sin living in me that does it. So I find this law at work: Although I want to do good, evil is right there with me. For in my inner being I delight in God's law; but I see another law at work in me, waging war against the law of my mind and making me a prisoner of the law of sin at work within me. What a wretched man I am! Who will rescue me from this body that is subject to death? Thanks be to God, who delivers me through Jesus Christ our Lord! So then, I myself in my mind am a slave to God's law, but in my sinful nature a slave to the law of sin (Romans 7:18:25 NIV).

As the following chapters make clear, we cannot overcome our sins and achieve our own salvation by performing good works or being on good behavior. Instead, salvation and the forgiveness of our sins are gifts from God. They are available only through his grace, in return for our belief in and acceptance of Jesus as his Son and our Savior.

The world may regard you, and you may regard yourself, as a good person. By the world's standards you probably are. For God's purposes, however, you are a sinner in need of redemption regardless of whether you also happen to be good in other ways.

Disciples:

All have sinned and fall short of the glory of God, and all are justified freely by his grace through the redemption that came by Christ Jesus. God presented Christ as a sacrifice of atonement, through the shedding of his blood—to be received by faith (Romans 3:23-25 NIV).

But Scripture has locked up everything under the control of sin, so that what was promised, being given through faith in Jesus Christ, might be given to those who believe (Galatians 3:22 NIV).

If we say, "We have no sin," we are deceiving ourselves, and the truth is not in us. If we confess our sins, he is faithful and righteous to forgive us our sins and to cleanse us from all unrighteousness. If we say, "We have not sinned," we make him a liar, and his word is not in us (1 John 1:8-10 CSB).

We must be cleansed of these sins to overcome their consequences and to become fit to enter God's presence. Our faith and belief that Jesus is our Savior cleanse us and allow us to overcome the natural consequences of sin and receive the salvation God offers.

Therefore, since we have been declared righteous by faith, we have peace with God through our Lord Jesus Christ. We have also obtained access through him by faith into this grace in which we stand, and we rejoice in the hope of the glory of God (Romans 5:1-2 CSB).

But where sin increased, grace increased all the more, so that, just as sin reigned in death, so also grace might reign through righteousness to bring eternal life through Jesus Christ our Lord (Romans 5:20-21 NIV).

But God, who is rich in mercy, because of his great love that he had for us, made us alive with Christ even though we were dead in trespasses. You are saved by grace! (Ephesians 2:4-5 CSB)

Let us approach with a true heart in full assurance of faith, with our hearts sprinkled clean from an evil conscience and our bodies washed with pure water. Let us hold fast to the confession of our hope without wavering, for he who has promised is faithful (Hebrews 10:22-23 NRSV).

But when the kindness of God our Savior and his love for mankind appeared, he saved us—not by works of righteousness that we had done, but according to his mercy—through the washing of regeneration and renewal by the Holy Spirit. He poured out his Spirit on us abundantly through Jesus Christ our Savior so that, having been justified by his grace, we may become heirs with the hope of eternal life (Titus 3:4-7 CSB).

My little children, I am writing these things to you so that you may not sin. But if anyone does sin, we have an advocate with the Father, Jesus Christ the righteous; and he is the atoning sacrifice for our sins, and not for ours only but also for the sins of the whole world (1 John 2:1-2 NRSV).

We now know that we need to become Christians to allow us to enter into a relationship with God despite our sinful nature. How do we go about doing that?

2

Believe

The first and most important thing you must do to become a Christian is believe that Jesus is the Son of God who came to earth to live and die to be your Savior. This book discusses many other things that factor into being sure you are a Christian, but none of them matters if you don't believe this.

Perhaps the clearest evidence that this belief in Jesus, and nothing else, is the source of salvation and eternal life is found in his words while he was being crucified. Next to him hung two criminals. One mocked and tested him. The other rebuked the first, and said, "Jesus, remember me when you come into your kingdom." Jesus answered him, "Truly I tell you, today you will be with me in Paradise" (Luke 23:39-43 CSB).

This person did nothing more than implicitly acknowledge his belief that Jesus was the Son of God, and in response, Jesus assured him that he would enter heaven. This proves, in Jesus' own words, that belief in Jesus is the exclusive source of salvation. The following passages are to the same effect.

Jesus:

"For God loved the world in this way: he gave his one and only Son, so that everyone who believes in him will not perish but have eternal life. For God did not send his Son into the world to condemn the world, but to save the world through him. Anyone who believes in him is not condemned, but anyone who does not believe is already condemned, because he has not believed in the name of the one and only Son of God" (John 3:16-18 CSB).

"And the Father who sent me has himself testified concerning me. You have never heard his voice nor seen his form, nor does

his word dwell in you, for you do not believe the one he sent" (John 5:37-38 NIV).

Jesus replied, "This is the work of God—that you believe in the one he has sent" (John 6:29 CSB).

"I am the bread of life. Whoever comes to me will never be hungry, and whoever believes in me will never be thirsty" (John 6:35 NRSV).

On the last and most important day of the festival, Jesus stood up and cried out, "If anyone is thirsty, let him come to me and drink. The one who believes in me, as the Scripture has said, will have streams of living water flow from deep within him" (John 7:37-38 CSB).

"You are from below; I am from above. You are of this world; I am not of this world. I told you that you would die in your sins; if you do not believe that I am he, you will indeed die in your sins" (John 8:23-24 NIV).

Referring to a blind man Jesus healed and the Pharisees chastised,

Jesus heard that they had thrown the man out, and when he found him, he asked, "Do you believe in the Son of Man?" "Who is he, Sir, that I may believe in him?" he asked. Jesus answered, "You have seen him; in fact, he is the one speaking with you." "I believe, Lord!" he said, and he worshiped him (John 9:35-38 CSB).

"Why then do you accuse me of blasphemy because I said, "I am God's Son"? Do not believe me unless I do the works of my Father. But if I do them, even though you do not believe me, believe the works, that you may know and understand that the Father is in me, and I in the Father (John 10:36-38 NIV).

Addressing Martha, sister of deceased Lazarus, before he raised Lazarus from the dead, Jesus asked,

"Didn't I tell you that if you believed you would see the glory of God?" So they removed the stone. Then Jesus raised his eyes and

said, *"Father, I thank you that you heard me. I know that you al-*
ways hear me, but because of the crowd standing here I said this,
so that they may believe you sent me" (John 11:40-42 CSB).

Then Jesus cried aloud: "Whoever believes in me believes not in
me but in him who sent me. And whoever sees me sees him who
sent me. I have come as light into the world, so that everyone
who believes in me should not remain in the darkness" (John
12:44-46 NRSV).

"I am telling you now before it happens, so that when it does
happen you will believe that I am who I am. Very truly I tell you,
whoever accepts anyone I send accepts me; and whoever accepts
me accepts the one who sent me" (John 13:19-20 NIV).

"I am the way and the truth and the life. No one comes to the
Father except through me" (John 14:6 NRSV).

"Don't you believe that I am in the Father and the Father is in
me? The words I speak to you I do not speak on my own. The
Father who lives in me does his works. Believe me that I am in
the Father and the Father is in me. Otherwise, believe because of
the works themselves" (John 14:10-11 CSB).

"No, the Father himself loves you because you have loved me
and have believed that I came from God. I came from the Father
and entered the world; now I am leaving the world and going
back to the Father." Then Jesus' disciples said, "Now you are
speaking clearly and without figures of speech. Now we can see
that you know all things and that you do not even need to have
anyone ask you questions. This makes us believe that you came
from God." "Do you now believe?" Jesus replied (John 16:27-31
NIV).

"I pray not only for these, but also for those who believe in me
through their word. May they all be one, as you, Father, are in
me and I am in you. May they also be in us, so that the world
may believe you sent me. I have given them the glory you have
given me, so that they may be one as we are one. I am in them

and you are in me, so that they may be made completely one, that the world may know you have sent me and have loved them as you have loved me (John 17:20-23 CSB).

Then he said to Thomas, "Put your finger here and see my hands. Reach out your hand and put it in my side. Do not doubt but believe." Thomas answered him, "My Lord and my God!" Jesus said to him, "Have you believed because you have seen me? Blessed are those who have not seen and yet have come to believe" (John 20:27-29 NRSV).

Disciples:

For Christ is the end of the law so that there may be righteousness for everyone who believes (Romans 10:4 NRSV).

Everyone who believes that Jesus is the Christ has been born of God, and everyone who loves the Father also loves the one born of him (1 John 5:1 CSB).

Who is it that conquers the world but the one who believes that Jesus is the Son of God? (1 John 5:5 NRSV)

All of the above verses make it clear that believing in Jesus is essential to salvation. That is true, and the rest of this book takes for granted that it is true. But what do you make of the following verse?

For this reason we labor and strive, because we have put our hope in the living God, who is the Savior of all people, especially of those who believe (1 Timothy 4:10 CSB).

This verse states, first, that God is the Savior of *all* people. It then says that God is *especially* the Savior of those who believe. How does one harmonize this verse with those quoted before it?

This is an example of an exercise that all Christians must engage in as they explore their faith and become more comfortable with it: harmonize seemingly inconsistent verses. I encourage you to do that through prayer, research, and consultation with your priest or pastor. Because there is a wide range of opinions about how many conflicting verses should be harmonized, I do not presume to pick the winner or go through that exercise for you here.

Let's return to what the Bible says about how you become a Christian. We know you must believe in Jesus. But what, exactly, does believing in Jesus do?

3

What Believing Does

Believing in Jesus, and thereby forming a relationship with God, has several results. Some verses describe the result as being "saved" from the consequences of sin, others as receiving "eternal life." Some describe it as providing "forgiveness of sins," and still others as allowing Christians to enter the "kingdom of God" or the "kingdom of heaven." Whatever the subtle differences between these results, we obviously want them all.

Believing Saves You

Jesus:

"You will be hated by everyone because of my name, but the one who endures to the end will be saved" (Mark 13:13 CSB).

Then he said to them, "Go into all the world and preach the gospel to all creation. Whoever believes and is baptized will be saved, but whoever does not believe will be condemned" (Mark 16:15-16 CSB).

And he said to the woman, "Your faith has saved you; go in peace" (Luke 7:50 NRSV).

"This is the meaning of the parable: The seed is the word of God. The seed along the path are those who have heard and then the devil comes and takes away the word from their hearts, so that they may not believe and be saved" (Luke 8:11-12 CSB).

For God did not send his Son into the world to condemn the world, but to save the world through him (John 3:17 NIV).

"I don't receive human testimony, but I say these things so that you may be saved" (John 5:34 CSB).

"If you hold to my teaching, you are really my disciples. Then you'll know the truth, and the truth will set you free" (John 8:31-32 NIV).

"I am the gate; whoever enters through me will be saved" (John 10:9 NRSV).

Disciples:

The angel of the Lord, who appeared to Joseph in a dream to explain Mary's pregnancy, said:

"She will give birth to a son, and you are to give him the name Jesus, because he will save his people from their sins" (Matthew 1:21 NIV).

Then everyone who calls on the name of the Lord will be saved (Acts 2:21 NRSV).

There is salvation in no one else, for there is no other name under heaven given to people by which we must be saved (Acts 4:12 CSB).

We believe it is through the grace of our Lord Jesus that we are saved (Acts 15:11 NIV).

Believe in the Lord Jesus, and you will be saved, you and your household (Acts 16:31 NRSV).

For I am not ashamed of the gospel, because it is the power of God for salvation to everyone who believes, first to the Jew, and also to the Greek (Romans 1:16 CSB).

But what does it say? "The word is near you: on your lips and in your heart" (that is, the word of faith that we proclaim); because if you confess with your lips that Jesus is Lord and believe in your heart that God raised him from the dead, you will be saved. For one believes with the heart and so is justified, and one confesses with the mouth and so is saved. The scripture says, "No one who believes in him will be put to shame." For there is no distinction between Jew and Greek; the same Lord is Lord of all and is generous to all who call on him. For, "Everyone who calls on the name of the Lord shall be saved" (Romans 10:8-13 NRSV).

For since, in God's wisdom, the world did not know God through wisdom, God was pleased to save those who believe through the foolishness of what is preached (1 Corinthians 1:21 CSB).

For I am not seeking my own good but the good of many, so that they may be saved. Follow my example, as I follow the example of Christ (1 Corinthians 10:33-11:1 NIV).

By this gospel you are saved, if you hold firmly to the word I preached to you. Otherwise, you have believed in vain. For what I received I passed on to you as of first importance: that Christ died for our sins according to the Scriptures, that he was buried, that he was raised on the third day according to the Scriptures (1 Corinthians 15:2-4 NIV).

In him you also were sealed with the promised Holy Spirit when you heard the word of truth, the gospel of your salvation, and when you believed (Ephesians 1:13 CSB).

You are saved by grace (Ephesians 2:5 CSB).

They displease God and are hostile to everyone in their effort to keep us from speaking to the Gentiles so that they may be saved (1 Thessalonians 2:15-16 NIV).

For God did not appoint us to wrath, but to obtain salvation through our Lord Jesus Christ, who died for us, so that whether we are awake or asleep, we may live together with him (1 Thessalonians 5:9-10 CSB).

But we ought to thank God always for you, brothers and sisters loved by the Lord, because from the beginning God has chosen you for salvation through sanctification by the Spirit and through belief in the truth (2 Thessalonians 2:13 CSB).

Christ Jesus came into the world to save sinners—of whom I am the worst (1 Timothy 1:15 NIV).

...that we may lead a tranquil and quiet life in all godliness and dignity. This is good, and it pleases God our Savior, who wants everyone to be saved and to come to the knowledge of the truth (1 Timothy 2:2-4 CSB).

But join with me in suffering for the gospel, relying on the power of God, who saved us and called us with a holy calling (2 Timothy 1:8-9 NRSV).

This salvation, which was first announced by the Lord, was confirmed to us by those who heard him. God also testified to it by signs, wonders and various miracles, and by gifts of the Holy Spirit distributed according to his will (Hebrews 2: 3-4 NIV).

And just as it is appointed for people to die once—and after this, judgment—so also Christ, having been offered once to bear the sins of many, will appear a second time, not to bear sin, but to bring salvation to those who are waiting for him (Hebrews 9:27-28 CSB).

Whoever turns a sinner from the error of his way will save his soul from death and cover a multitude of sins (James 5:20 CSB).

Though you have not seen him, you love him; and even though you do not see him now, you believe in him and are filled with an inexpressible and glorious joy, for you are receiving the end result of your faith, the salvation of your souls (1 Peter 1:8-9 NIV).

Believing Gives You Eternal Life

Jesus:

"And they will go away into eternal punishment, but the righteous into eternal life" (Matthew 25:46 CSB).

"And just as Moses lifted up the serpent in the wilderness, so must the Son of Man be lifted up, that whoever believes in him may have eternal life. For God so loved the world that he gave

his only Son, so that everyone who believes in him may not perish but may have eternal life" (John 3:14-16 NRSV).

"The one who believes in the Son has eternal life, but the one who rejects the Son will not see life; instead the wrath of God remains on him" (John 3:36 CSB).

"But whoever drinks the water I give them will never thirst. Indeed, the water I give them will become to them a spring of water welling up to eternal life" (John 4:14 NIV).

"Truly I tell you, anyone who hears my word and believes him who sent me has eternal life and will not come under judgment but has passed from death to life" (John 5:24 CSB).

"Don't work for the food that perishes but for the food that lasts for eternal life, which the Son of Man will give you, because God the Father has set his seal of approval on him" (John 6:27 CSB).

"It is the spirit that gives life; the flesh is useless. The words that I have spoken to you are spirit and life" (John 6:63 NRSV).

"For my Father's will is that everyone who looks to the Son and believes in him shall have eternal life, and I will raise them up at the last day" (John 6:40 NIV).

"Truly I tell you, anyone who believes has eternal life. I am the bread of life. Your ancestors ate the manna in the wilderness, and they died. This is the bread that comes down from heaven so that anyone may eat of it and not die. I am the living bread that came down from heaven. If anyone eats of this bread he will live forever. The bread that I will give for the life of the world is my flesh" (John 6:47-51 CSB).

"I am the light of the world. Anyone who follows me will never walk in the darkness but will have the light of life" (John 8:12 CSB).

"Truly I tell you, if anyone keeps my word, he will never see death" (John 8:51 CSB).

Jesus answered, "I have told you, and you do not believe. The works that I do in my Father's name testify to me; but you do not believe, because you do not belong to my sheep. My sheep hear my voice. I know them, and they follow me. I give them eternal life, and they will never perish. No one will snatch them out of my hand" (John 10:25-28 NRSV).

Jesus said to her, "I am the resurrection and the life. The one who believes in me, even if he dies, will live. Everyone who lives and believes in me will never die" (John 11:25-26 CSB).

"For I did not speak on my own, but the Father who sent me commanded me what to say all that I have spoken. I know that his command leads to eternal life. So whatever I say is just what the Father has told me to say" (John 12:49-50 NIV).

Jesus spoke these things, looked up to heaven, and said: "Father, the hour has come. Glorify your Son so that the Son may glorify you, since you gave him authority over all flesh, so that he may give eternal life to everyone you have given him" (John 17:1-2 CSB).

Disciples:

Simon Peter answered him, "Lord, to whom can we go? You have the words of eternal life. We have come to believe and know that you are the Holy One of God" (John 6:68-69 NRSV).

Jesus performed many other signs in the presence of his disciples, which are not recorded in this book. But these are written that you may believe that Jesus is the Messiah, the Son of God, and that by believing you may have life in his name (John 20:30-31 NIV).

So that, just as sin exercised dominion in death, so grace might also exercise dominion through justification leading to eternal life through Jesus Christ our Lord (Romans 5:21 NRSV).

For the wages of sin is death, but the gift of God is eternal life in Christ Jesus our Lord (Romans 6:23 CSB).

But for that very reason I was shown mercy so that in me, the worst of sinners, Christ Jesus might display his immense patience as an example for those who would believe on him and receive eternal life (1 Timothy 1:16 NIV).

The one who believes in the Son of God has this testimony within himself. The one who does not believe God has made him a liar, because he has not believed in the testimony God has given about his Son. And this is the testimony: God has given us eternal life, and this life is in his Son (1 John 5:10-11 CSB).

I write these things to you who believe in the name of the Son of God so that you may know that you have eternal life (1 John 5:13 NRSV).

Believing Makes You Part of the Kingdom

Jesus:

"Blessed are the poor in spirit, for the kingdom of heaven is theirs" (Matthew 5:3 CSB).

"Not everyone who says to me, 'Lord, Lord' will enter the kingdom of heaven, but only the one who does the will of my Father who is in heaven" (Matthew 7:21 NIV).

"Truly I tell you, among those born of women no greater than John the Baptist has appeared, but the least in the kingdom of heaven is greater than he. From the days of John the Baptist until now, the kingdom of heaven has been suffering violence, and the violent have been seizing it by force" (Matthew 11:11-12 CSB).

"Because the knowledge of the secrets of the kingdom of heaven has been given to you, but not to them" (Matthew 13:11 NIV).

"When anyone hears the word about the kingdom and doesn't

understand it, the evil one comes and snatches away what was sown in his heart" (Matthew 13:19 CSB).

"The kingdom of heaven is like a man who sowed good seed in his field. But while everyone was sleeping, his enemy came and sowed weeds among the wheat, and went away" (Matthew 13:24-25 NIV).

"The kingdom of heaven is like a mustard seed that a man took and sowed in his field. It's the smallest of all the seeds, but when grown, it's taller than the garden plants and becomes a tree, so that the birds of the sky come and nest in its branches" (Matthew 13:31-32 CSB).

"The kingdom of heaven is like yeast that a woman took and mixed in with three measures of flour until all of it was unleavened" (Matthew 13:33 NRSV).

"The kingdom of heaven is like treasure, buried in a field, that a man found and reburied. Then in his joy he goes and sells everything he has and buys that field. Again, the kingdom of heaven is like a merchant in search of fine pearls. When he found one priceless pearl, he went and sold everything he had and bought it. Again, the kingdom of heaven is like a large net thrown into the sea. It collected every kind of fish and when it was full, they dragged it ashore, sat down, and gathered the good fish into containers, but threw out the worthless ones" (Matthew 13:44-48 CSB).

"Therefore every scribe who has been trained for the kingdom of heaven is like the master of a household who brings out of his treasure what is new and what is old" (Matthew 13:52 NRSV).

"I will give you the keys of the kingdom of heaven, and whatever you bind on earth will have been bound in heaven, and whatever you loose on earth will have been loosed in heaven" (Matthew 16:19 CSB).

"Therefore, the kingdom of heaven is like a king who wanted to

settle accounts with his servants" (Matthew 18:23 NIV).

"Again I tell you, it is easier for a camel to go through the eye of a needle than for a rich person to enter the kingdom of God" (Matthew 19:24 CSB).

"Therefore I tell you that the kingdom of God will be taken away from you and given to a people who will produce its fruit" (Matthew 21:43 NIV).

"And if your eye causes you to stumble, tear it out; it is better for you to enter the kingdom of God with one eye than to have two eyes and to be thrown into hell" (Mark 9:47 NRSV).

"Let the little children come to me. Don't stop them, because the kingdom of God belongs to such as these. Truly I tell you, whoever does not receive the kingdom of God like a little child will never enter it" (Mark 10:14-15 CSB).

"How hard it is for the rich to enter the kingdom of God!" The disciples were amazed at his words. But Jesus said again, "Children, how hard it is to enter the kingdom of God! It is easier for a camel to go through the eye of a needle than for someone who is rich to enter the kingdom of God" (Mark 10:23-25 NIV).

But he said to them, "I must proclaim the good news of the kingdom of God to the other cities also; for I was sent for this purpose" (Luke 4:43 NRSV).

"Heal the sick who are there, and tell them, 'The kingdom of God has come near you'" (Luke 10:9 CSB).

"The kingdom of God is not coming with things that can be observed; nor will they say, 'Look, here it is!' or 'There it is!' For, in fact, the kingdom of God is among you" (Luke 17:20-21 NRSV).

"Very truly I tell you, no one can see the kingdom of God unless they are born again... Very truly I tell you, no one can enter the kingdom of God unless they are born of water and the Spirit.

Flesh gives birth to flesh, but the Spirit gives birth to spirit" (John 3:3, 5-6 NIV).

Disciples:

Repent, because the kingdom of heaven has come near! (Matthew 3:2 CSB)

Do you not know that wrongdoers will not inherit the kingdom of God? (1 Corinthians 6:9 NRSV)

Believing Forgives Your Sins

Jesus:

And after getting into a boat he crossed the sea and came to his own town. And just then some people were carrying a paralyzed man lying on a bed. When Jesus saw their faith, he said to the paralytic, "Take heart, son; your sins are forgiven." Then some of the scribes said to themselves, "This man is blaspheming." But Jesus, perceiving their thoughts, said, "Why do you think evil in your hearts? For which is easier, to say, 'Your sins are forgiven,' or to say, 'Stand up and walk'? But so that you may know that the Son of Man has authority on earth to forgive sins"—he then said to the paralytic—"Stand up, take your bed and go to your home" (Matthew 9:1-6 NRSV).

"Therefore I tell you, her many sins have been forgiven; that's why she loved much. But the one who is forgiven little, loves little." Then he said to her, "Your sins are forgiven" (Luke 7:47-48 CSB).

"I am sending you to them to open their eyes so that they may turn from darkness to light and from the power of Satan to God, that they may receive forgiveness of sins and a share among those who are sanctified by faith in me" (Acts 26:17-18 CSB).

Disciples:

God exalted this man to his right hand as ruler and Savior, to give repentance to Israel and forgiveness of sins (Acts 5:31 CSB).

All the prophets testify about him that everyone who believes in him receives forgiveness of sins through his name (Acts 10:43 NIV).

Therefore, let it be known to you, brothers and sisters, that through this man forgiveness of sins is being proclaimed to you. Everyone who believes is justified through him from everything that you could not be justified from through the law of Moses (Acts 13:38 CSB).

Therefore, there is now no condemnation for those in Christ Jesus, because the law of the Spirit of life in Christ Jesus has set you free from the law of sin and death (Romans 8:1-2 CSB).

In him we have redemption through his blood, the forgiveness of sins, in accordance with the riches of God's grace that he lavished on us (Ephesians 1:7-8 NIV).

In him we have redemption, the forgiveness of sins (Colossians 1:14 CSB).

Once you were alienated and hostile in your minds expressed in your evil actions. But now he has reconciled you by his physical body through his death, to present you holy, faultless, and blameless before him—if indeed you remain grounded and steadfast in the faith and are not shifted away from the hope of the gospel that you heard (Colossians 1:21-23 CSB).

He forgive us all our sins, having canceled the charge of our legal indebtedness, which stood against us and condemned us; he has taken it away, nailing it to the cross (Colossians 2:13-14 NIV).

Just as the Lord has forgiven you, so you are also to forgive

(Colossians 3:13 CSB).

If we confess our sins, he who is faithful and just will forgive us our sins and cleanse us from all unrighteousness (1 John 1:9 NRSV).

I am writing to you, dear children, because your sins have been forgiven on account of his name (1 John 2:12 NIV).

Believing in Jesus, also described as having faith in him, is such a simple thing, but it is the most important and rewarding thing you will ever do. Its results are incomparable. It saves you from eternal damnation and gives you eternal life. It causes God to forgive your sins and makes you a member of his kingdom. As the next chapter makes clear, it is critical that you believe in Jesus because doing so is not just a way to achieve these things—it is the *only* way.

4

Faith and Grace, Not Works

Jesus and his followers describe faith in Jesus as essential to salvation; it is what procures God's grace and our salvation. But what is faith?

Faith is confidence in what we hope for and assurance about what we do not see (Hebrews 11:1 NIV).

And without faith it is impossible to please God, because anyone who comes to him must believe that he exists and that he rewards those who earnestly seek him (Hebrews 11:6 NIV).

When Paul recounted his conversion on the road to Damascus and Jesus' instructions that he spread Jesus' message throughout the world, he quoted Jesus as saying that those who have faith in Jesus are "sanctified" by that faith:

"I am sending you to them to open their eyes so that they may turn from darkness to light and from the power of Satan to God, that they may receive forgiveness of sins and a share among those who are sanctified by faith in me" (Acts 26:17-18 CSB).

Many passages in the New Testament emphasize the critical role that faith and the grace it procures play in the life of Christians and their relationship to God.

Disciples:

For in [the gospel] the righteousness of God is revealed through faith for faith; as it is written, "The one who is righteous will live by faith" (Romans 1:17 NRSV).

But now, apart from the law, the righteousness of God has been revealed, attested by the Law and the Prophets. The righteousness of God is through faith in Jesus Christ to all who believe, since there is no distinction. For all have sinned and fall short of the glory of God. They are justified freely by his grace through the redemption that is in Christ Jesus. God presented him as an atoning sacrifice in his blood, received through faith, to demonstrate his righteousness, because in his restraint God passed over the sins previously committed. God presented him to demonstrate his righteousness at the present time, so that he would be righteous and declare righteous the one who has faith in Jesus (Romans 3:21-26 CSB).

For we maintain that a person is justified by faith apart from the works of the law...[T]here is only one God, who will justify the circumcised by faith and the uncircumcised through that same faith (Romans 3:28,30 NIV).

This is why the promise is by faith, so that it may be according to grace, to guarantee it to all the descendants—not only to those who are of the law but also to those who are of Abraham's faith. He is the father of us all (Romans 4:16 CSB).

Therefore, since we are justified by faith, we have peace with God through our Lord Jesus Christ, through whom we have obtained access to this grace in which we stand (Romans 5:1-2 NRSV).

Therefore we are always confident and know that as long as we are at home in the body we are away from the Lord. We live by faith, not by sight (2 Corinthians 5:6-7 NIV).

I have been crucified with Christ, and I no longer live, but Christ lives in me. The life I now live in the body, I live by faith in the son of God, who loved me and gave himself for me (Galatians 2:20 CSB).

Clearly no one is justified before God by the law, because, "The righteous will live by faith" (Galatians 3:11 NIV).

The purpose was that the blessing of Abraham would come to the Gentiles by Christ Jesus, so that we could receive the promised Spirit through faith (Galatians 3:14 CSB).

But the scripture has imprisoned all things under the power of sin, so that what was promised through faith in Jesus Christ might be given to those who believe. Now before faith came, we were imprisoned and guarded under the law until faith would be revealed. Therefore the law was our disciplinarian until Christ came, so that we might be justified by faith. But now that faith has come, we are no longer subject to a disciplinarian, for in Christ Jesus you are all children of God through faith (Galatians 3:22-26 NRSV).

You who are trying to be justified by the law are alienated from Christ; you have fallen from grace. For we eagerly await through the Spirit, by faith, the hope of righteousness. For in Christ Jesus neither circumcision nor uncircumcision accomplishes anything; what matters is faith working through love (Galatians 5:4-6 CSB).

I pray that out of his glorious riches he may strengthen you with power through his Spirit in your inner being, so that Christ may dwell in your hearts through faith (Ephesians 3:16-17 NIV).

Because of him I have suffered the loss of all things and consider them as dung, so that I may gain Christ and be found in him, not having a righteousness of my own from the law, but one that is through faith in Christ—the righteousness from God based on faith (Philippians 8:9-10 CSB).

In him also you were circumcised with a spiritual circumcision, by putting off the body of the flesh in the circumcision of Christ; when you were buried with him in baptism, you were also raised with him through faith in the power of God, who raised him from the dead (Colossians 2:11-12 NRSV).

These promote empty speculations rather than God's plan, which operates by faith. Now the goal of our instruction is love that comes from a pure heart, a good conscience, and a sincere faith (1 Timothy 1:4-5 CSB).

And without faith it is impossible to please God, because anyone who comes to him must believe that he exists and that he rewards those who earnestly seek him (Hebrews 11:6 NIV).

You rejoice in this, even though now for a short time, if necessary, you suffer grief in various trials so that the proven character of your faith—more valuable than gold which, though perishable, is refined by fire—may result in praise, glory, and honor at the revelation of Jesus Christ. Though you have not seen him, you love him; though not seeing him now, you believe in him, and you rejoice with inexpressible and glorious joy because you are receiving the goal of your faith, the salvation of your souls (1 Peter 1:6-9 CSB).

Good Works Will Not Save You

Spoiler Alert: there is a relationship between your conduct and being a Christian, which is what much of this book is about. That relationship is one of cause and effect. But it is critical to understand which is the cause and which is the effect.

Good conduct is not a cause, and being a Christian is not an effect. In other words, being on good behavior and doing good things does not make you a Christian.

This should be pretty obvious. Christians do not have a monopoly on good behavior. Many non-believers, atheists, and people of other faiths do good things but, according to the New Testament, those good things do not create a personal relationship with God that will procure their salvation.

For example, although lawyers tend to read a lot and operate under a relatively high degree of stress, just because you read a lot and operate under a relatively high degree of stress does not mean you are a lawyer. Similarly, although happily married people tend not to go to bars to look for people to hook up with, just because you don't go to bars to look for people to hook up with does not mean you are happily married. Likewise, although Christians (should) tend to do good things, just because you do good things does not mean you are a Christian.

So why beat up such an obvious point? Because much of the rest of this book talks about the importance of good behavior in the life of a Christian, and many people react to that topic by saying, "But good behavior does not make you a Christian." Nothing in this book is intended to suggest that being on good behavior makes you a Christian. In fact, the notion that one may earn salvation by good works alone is antithetical to Jesus' message: that salvation is a gift from God that you receive by having faith that Jesus is God's Son and accepting Christ as your Savior.

Disciples:

Where, then, is boasting? It is excluded. By what kind of law? By one of works? No, on the contrary, by a law of faith. For we conclude that a person is justified by faith apart from the works of the law (Romans 3:27-28 CSB).

What then are we to say? Gentiles, who did not strive for righteousness, have attained it, that is, righteousness through faith; but Israel, who did strive for the righteousness that is based on the law, did not succeed in fulfilling that law. Why not? Because they did not strive for it on the basis of faith, but as if it were based on works. They have stumbled over the stumbling stone (Romans 9:30-32 NRSV).

In the same way, then, there is also at the present time a remnant chosen by grace. Now if by grace, then it is not by works; otherwise grace ceases to be grace (Romans 11 5-6 CSB).

For you are saved by grace through faith, and this is not from yourselves; it is God's gift—not from works, so that no one can boast (Ephesians 2:8-9 CSB).

But when the kindness and love of God our Savior appeared, he saved us, not because of righteous things we had done, but because of his mercy (Titus 3:4-5 NIV).

So, if good behavior is not the cause, and salvation not the effect, in this cause and effect relationship, you've probably already concluded that salvation is the cause and good behavior the effect. Congratulations! Much of the rest of this book addresses the importance of behavior in the spiritual life of a Christian and the role it plays in being sure you are a Christian. It plays a significant role, but it doesn't make you a Christian. Nor does following the Law of the Old Testament.

Following the Law Will Not Save You

Since Jesus became part of God's plan for having a relationship with people, obeying the Law set forth in the Old Testament is no longer sufficient to have that relationship. (The Law is contained in the first five books of the Old Testament; the Prophets make up the rest of the Old Testament. So, when the New Testament verses refer to "the Law and the Prophets," they are referring to teachings included in what we now call the Old Testament.)

This set of ideas and verses are an extension of the idea that good behavior, or good works, cannot overcome sin and allow a person to establish a relationship with God that will afford them salvation. It warrants separate discussion, however, because following the Law and the Prophets was, for millennia, the way people of God created and enjoyed that relationship. Those of the Jewish faith believe they still do. The New Testament refers to that state of affairs as "the Old Covenant," which was replaced by the relationship Jesus affords Christians, "the New Covenant."

For Christ is the end of the law for righteousness to everyone who believes (Romans 10:4 CSB).

He forgave us all our sins, having canceled the charge of our legal indebtedness, which stood against us and condemned us; he has taken it away, nailing it to the cross (Colossians 2:13-14 NIV).

Nonetheless, the Law still has an important role in God's plan of salvation. The New Testament contains many verses that address the role Old Testament teachings play in the life of a Christian and the

New Covenant. Perhaps the most important is that it makes us conscious of sin.

Therefore no one will be declared righteous in God's sight by the works of the law; rather, through the law we become conscious of our sin (Romans 3:20 NIV).

Beyond that, the following verses describe how the Old Covenant was fulfilled in the New Covenant as the way people may enjoy a personal relationship with God.

Disciples:

Therefore, let it be known to you, brothers and sisters, that through this man forgiveness of sins is being proclaimed to you. Everyone who believes is justified through him from everything that you could not be justified from through the law of Moses (Acts 13:38-39 CSB).

But now, apart from law, the righteousness of God has been disclosed, and is attested by the law and the prophets, the righteousness of God through faith in Jesus Christ for all who believe. For there is no distinction, since all have sinned and fall short of the glory of God; they are now justified by his grace as a gift, through the redemption that is in Christ Jesus, ...For we hold that a person is justified by faith apart from works prescribed by the law (Romans 3:21-24, 28 NRSV).

This is why the promise is by faith, so that it may be according to grace, to guarantee it to all the descendants—not only to those who are of the law but also to those who are of Abraham's faith. He is the father of us all (Romans 4:16 CSB).

We ourselves are Jews by birth and not Gentile sinners; yet we know that a person is justified not by the works of the law but through faith in Jesus Christ. And we have come to believe in Christ Jesus, so that we might be justified by faith in Christ, and not by doing the works of the law, because no one will be justified by the works of the law (Galatians 2:15-16 NRSV).

I only want to learn this from you: Did you receive the Spirit by the works of the law or by believing what you heard?... So then, does God give you the Spirit and work miracles among you by you are doing the works of the law? Or is it by believing what you heard? (Galatians 3:2, 5 CSB).

For all who rely on the works of the law are under a curse, because it is written, Everyone who does not do everything written in the book of the law is cursed. Now it is clear that no one is justified before God by the law, because the righteous will live by faith. But the law is not based on faith; instead the one who does these things will live by them. Christ redeemed us from the curse of the law by becoming a curse for us, because it is written, Cursed is everyone who is hung on a tree. The purpose was that the blessing of Abraham would come to the Gentiles by Christ Jesus, so that we could receive the promised Spirit through faith (Galatians 3:10-14 CSB).

Before the coming of this faith, we were held in custody under the law, locked up until the faith that was to come would be revealed. So the law was our guardian until Christ came that we might be justified by faith. Now that this faith has come, we are no longer under a guardian (Galatians 3:23-25 NIV).

You who are trying to be justified by the law are alienated from Christ; you have fallen from grace (Galatians 5:4 CSB).

There are many reasons to behave yourself and do good things. As we will see, whether you do good things and how you conduct yourself play a significant role in being sure you are a Christian. But doing good things and being on good behavior cannot, and will not, make you a Christian. Your conduct cannot earn salvation, forgiveness of sins, a place in God's kingdom, or eternal life. Only faith in Jesus, and the grace God extends to those who have that faith, can do that. As a bonus, that faith also gives you a spiritual helper: The Holy Spirit.

5

The Holy Spirit

When a person becomes a Christian, they receive the Holy Spirit.
God sent the Holy Spirit to dwell within Christians as the presence of
God in our lives and souls. As John the Baptist foretold before Jesus
began his ministry:

*I baptize you with water for repentance, but one who is more
powerful than I is coming after me; I am not worthy to carry his
sandals. He will baptize you with the Holy Spirit and fire*
(Matthew 3:11 NRSV).

[John the Baptist] *proclaimed, "One who is more powerful than I
am is coming after me. I am not worthy to stoop down and untie
the straps of his sandals. I baptize you with water, but he will
baptize you with the Holy Spirit"* (Mark 1:7-8 CSB).

Likewise, after Jesus was crucified and rose again, he gave his
disciples what is called "the Great Commission." The Great
Commission included Jesus' instruction:

*"Go, therefore, and make disciples of all nations, baptizing them
in the name of the Father and of the Son and of the Holy Spirit,
teaching them to observe everything I have commanded you"*
(Matthew 28:19-20 CSB).

During his ministry, Jesus explained that God would give the
Holy Spirit to Christians to provide them with the spiritual gifts he
promises.

*"If you then, though you are evil, know how to give good gifts to
your children, how much more will your Father in heaven give
the Holy Spirit to those who ask him!"* (Luke 11:13 NIV)

*On the last and greatest day of the festival, Jesus stood and said
in a loud voice, "Let anyone who is thirsty come to me and drink.*

Whoever believes in me, as the Scripture has said, streams of living water will flow from within them." By this he meant the Spirit, whom those who believed in him were later to receive. Up to that time the Spirit had not been given, since Jesus had not yet been glorified (John 7:37-39 NIV).

"I have spoken these things to you while I remain with you. But the Counselor, the Holy Spirit, whom the Father will send in my name, will teach you all things and remind you of everything I have told you" (John 14:25-26 CSB).

Just as Jesus promised, God gave the Holy Spirit to believers shortly after Jesus' death and resurrection during the 40 days when he was with them:

While he was with them, he commanded them not to leave Jerusalem, but to wait for the Father's promise. "Which," he said, "you have heard me speak about; for John baptized with water, but you will be baptized with the Holy Spirit in a few days....But you will receive power when the Holy Spirit has come on you, and you will be my witnesses in Jerusalem, and all Judea and Samaria, and to the end of the earth" (Acts 1:4,5,8 CSB).

When the day of Pentecost had come, they were all together in one place. And suddenly from heaven there came a sound like the rush of a violent wind, and it filled the entire house where they were sitting. Divided tongues, as of fire, appeared among them, and a tongue rested on each of them. All of them were filled with the Holy Spirit and began to speak in other languages, as the Spirit gave them ability (Acts 2:1-4 NRSV).

The Holy Spirit Dwells in Christians

Jesus promised the gift of the Holy Spirit. God delivered on that promise on Pentecost and has done so ever since.

Peter replied, "Repent and be baptized, each of you, in the name of Jesus Christ for the forgiveness of your sins, and you will receive the gift of the Holy Spirit. For the promise is for you and for your children, and for all who are far off, as many as the Lord our God will call" (Acts: 38-39 CSB).

This is a straightforward promise: all who believe in Jesus and are baptized in his name will receive the Holy Spirit. The Book of Acts contains a vivid description of the gift of the Holy Spirit being instantaneously bestowed upon a group of believers. This event was particularly dramatic to the disciples because it confirmed that Gentiles and Jews alike were eligible to be saved and to be baptized.

While Peter was still speaking these words, the Holy Spirit came on all who heard the message. The circumcised believers who had come with Peter were astonished that the gift of the Holy Spirit had been poured out even on the Gentiles. For they heard them speaking in tongues and praising God. Then Peter said, "Surely no one can stand in the way of their being baptized with water. They have received the Holy Spirit just as we have" (Acts 10:44-47 NIV).

A number of other verses contain assurances that the Holy Spirit dwells within all who become Christians.

Jesus:

"Whoever believes in me, as the Scripture has said, rivers of living water will flow from within them." By this he meant the Spirit, whom those who believed in him were later to receive. Up to that time the Spirit had not been given, since Jesus had not yet been glorified (John 7:38-39 NIV).

"When the Counselor comes, the one I will send to you from the Father—the Spirit of truth who proceeds from the Father—he will testify about me" (John 15:26 CSB).

Disciples:

John answered all of them by saying, "I baptize you with water; but one who is more powerful than I is coming; I am not worthy to untie the thongs of his sandals. He will baptize you with the

Holy Spirit and fire" (Luke 3:16 NRSV).

We are witnesses of these things, and so is the Holy Spirit whom God has given to those who obey him (Acts 5:32 CSB).

The Spirit himself testifies with our spirit that we are God's children (Romans 8:16 NIV).

Do you not know that your bodies are temples of the Holy Spirit, who is in you, whom you have received from God? (1 Corinthians 6:19 NIV).

I only want to learn this from you: Did you receive the Spirit by the works of the law or by believing what you heard? Are you so foolish? After beginning by the Spirit are you now finishing by the flesh? Did you experience so much for nothing—if in fact it was for nothing? So then, does God give you the Spirit and work miracles among you by your doing the works of the law? Or is it by believing what you heard (Ephesians 3:2-5 CSB).

In him you also, when you had heard the word of truth, the gospel of your salvation, and had believed in him, were marked with the seal of the promised Holy Spirit; this is the pledge of our inheritance toward redemption as God's own people, to the praise of his glory (Ephesians 1:13-14 NRSV).

The Holy Spirit Marks and Empowers Christians

The Holy Spirit plays a vital role in the lives of Christians. The Scriptures say that he gives us life, helps us understand God and his teachings, is the source of the gift of prophecy and power, is a marker of Christians, and, most importantly for purposes of this book, "controls" Christians.

Jesus:

"When you are brought before synagogues, rulers and authorities, do not worry about how you will defend yourselves or what you will say, for the Holy Spirit will teach you at that time what

you should say" (Luke 12:11-12 NIV).

"I have spoken these things to you while I remain with you. But the Counselor, the Holy Spirit, whom the Father will send in my name, will teach you all things and remind you of everything I have told you" (John 14:25-26 CSB).

"When the Spirit of truth comes, he will guide you into all the truth; for he will not speak on his own, but will speak whatever he hears, and he will declare to you the things that are to come. He will glorify me, because he will take what is mine and declare it to you. All that the Father has is mine. For this reason I said that he will take what is mine and declare it to you" (John 16:13-15 NRSV).

"But you will receive power when the Holy Spirit comes on you; and you will be my witnesses in Jerusalem, and in all Judea and Samaria, and to the ends of the earth" (Acts 1:8 NIV).

Disciples:

When they had prayed, the place where they were assembled was shaken, and they were all filled with the Holy Spirit and began to speak the word of God boldly (Acts 4:31 CSB).

But you are not in the flesh; you are in the Spirit, since the Spirit of God dwells in you. Anyone who does not have the Spirit of Christ does not belong to him (Romans 8:9 NRSV).

And if the Spirit of him who raised Jesus from the dead lives in you, then he who raised Christ from the dead will also bring your mortal bodies to life through his Spirit who lives in you (Romans 8:11 CSB).

Likewise the Spirit helps us in our weakness; for we do not know how to pray as we ought, but that very Spirit intercedes with sighs too deep for words. And God, who searches the heart, knows what is the mind of the Spirit, because the Spirit inter-cedes for the saints according to the will of God (Romans 8:26-

27 NRSV).

But, as it is written, "What no eye has seen, nor ear heard, nor the human heart conceived, what God has prepared for those who love him"— these things God has revealed to us through the Spirit; for the Spirit searches everything, even the depths of God. For what human being knows what is truly human except the human spirit that is within? So also no one comprehends what is truly God's except the Spirit of God. Now we have received not the spirit of the world, but the Spirit that is from God, so that we may understand the gifts bestowed on us by God. And we speak of these things in words not taught by human wisdom but taught by the Spirit, interpreting spiritual things to those who are spiritual. Those who are unspiritual do not receive the gifts of God's Spirit, for they are foolishness to them, and they are unable to understand them because they are spiritually discerned (1 Corinthians 2:9-14 NRSV).

I say then, walk by the Spirit and you will certainly not carry out the desire of the flesh. For the flesh desires what is against the Spirit, and the Spirit desires what is against the flesh; these are opposed to each other, so that you don't do what you want. But if you are led by the Spirit, you are not under the law (Galatians 5:16-17 CSB).

Above all, you know this: No prophecy of Scripture comes from the prophet's own interpretation, because no prophecy ever came by the will of man; instead, men spoke from God as they were carried along by the Holy Spirit (2 Peter 20:21 CSB).

Acts contains two accounts of groups of people becoming Christians that are particularly instructive for purposes of this book. The first account relates to a group of what Acts describes as "disciples" Paul found in Ephesus:

He found some disciples and asked them, "Did you receive the Holy Spirit when you believed?" "No," they told him, "we haven't even heard that there is a Holy Spirit." "Into what then were you baptized?" he asked them. "Into John's baptism," they replied. Paul said, "John baptized with a baptism of repentance, telling the people that they should believe in the one who would come after him, that is, in Jesus." When they heard this, they were baptized into the name of the Lord Jesus. And when Paul had laid his hands on them, the Holy Spirit came on them, and they began to speak in other tongues and to prophecy (Acts 19:1-6 CSB).

Three important things jump out of this account. First, as explained more fully in Chapter 6, repentance is an important part of becoming a Christian but is not sufficient to become a Christian. Second, whatever this group of people believed that caused Luke (the author of Acts) to call them "disciples," they had not learned that they had to believe in Jesus. Once they did, they proclaimed their belief in him through baptism in Jesus. Third, and curiously, they apparently did not receive the Holy Spirit upon professing their belief in Jesus; they received the Holy Spirit only when Paul laid his hands on them.

The third point is of concern because: (i) the verses quoted above make it clear that the Holy Spirit dwells within Christians and is in fact a marker of Christians; but (ii) although these people did what it takes to become Christians (profess their belief in Jesus), the Holy Spirit did not come upon them until Paul laid his hands on them. Why? And what about us, who do not have Paul around?

The second account is even more troubling for those who want certainty about their status as Christians. It concerns a group of people in Samaria who "accepted the word of God" and were baptized, but they still did not receive the Holy Spirit.

When the apostles in Jerusalem heard that Samaria had accepted the word of God, they sent Peter and John to Samaria. When they arrived, they prayed for the new believers that they might receive the Holy Spirit, because the Holy Spirit had not yet come on any of them; they had simply been baptized in the name of the Lord Jesus. Then Peter and John placed their hands on them, and they received the Holy Spirit (Acts 8:14-17 NIV).

Luke, how about a little more information? How could these people have accepted the word of God and been baptized in the name of the Lord Jesus, yet not have received the Holy Spirit? We know what the group of Ephesians in the first account lacked; they subscribed only to John the Baptist's teaching of repentance. They missed half the story. This account of the Samaritans does not tell us what part of the story they missed.

Whatever it was, these passages help people who want to be certain they are Christians focus their attention on a simple truth: You can get this wrong. This highlights the importance of having a clear understanding of what it takes to be sure you are a Christian.

So far, we have learned that, to become a Christian, you must believe and have faith that Jesus, God's Son, died on the cross to save you from your sins and give you eternal life in God's kingdom. Many verses suggest that is enough; perhaps it is.

But other verses, which we are about to cover, suggest the controversial ideas, seemingly contradicted by other verses, that you must repent, that you must forgive others, and even that God must choose you for you to become a Christian. These verses are among the many you must make peace with to be sure you are a Christian. The first step in doing that is to read and prayerfully consider them, and then turn to research and a member of the clergy for guidance about your verse-specific questions and concerns.

6

Must You Repent?

Webster's New World College Dictionary (Fourth Edition) defines "repent" as "to feel so contrite over one's sins as to change, or decide to change, one's ways; be penitent." Biblically, think of repentance as changing your mind in a way that changes your actions.

In some verses, Jesus and his disciples describe repentance as an integral, necessary aspect of becoming a Christian and being saved—in addition to believing in Jesus. In other verses, the instruction to repent is clear, but the consequences of not doing so are not. The following verses suggest that repentance is a necessary part of being saved:

Jesus:

At that time, some people came and reported to him about the Galileans whose blood Pilate mixed with their sacrifices. And he responded to them, "Do you think that these Galileans were more sinful than all the other Galileans because they suffered these things? No, I tell you; but unless you repent, you will all perish as well. Or those eighteen that the tower in Siloam fell on and killed—do you think they were more sinful than all the other people who live in Jerusalem? No, I tell you; but unless you repent, you will all perish as well" (Luke 13:1-5 CSB).

Disciples:

Jesus began to denounce the towns in which most of his miracles had been performed, because they did not repent (Matthew 11:20 NIV).

Peter replied, "Repent and be baptized, each of you, in the name of Jesus Christ for the forgiveness of your sins, and you will receive the gift of the Holy Spirit" (Acts 2:38 CSB).

Repent, then, and turn to God, so that your sins may be wiped out, that times of refreshing may come from the Lord, and that he may send the Messiah, who has been appointed for you—even Jesus (Acts 3:19-20 NIV).

When Simon saw that the Spirit was given through the laying on of the apostles' hands, he offered them money, saying, "Give me this power also so that anyone I lay hands on may receive the Holy Spirit." But Peter told him, "May your silver be destroyed with you, because you thought you could obtain the gift of God with money! You have no part or share in this matter, because your heart is not right before God. Therefore repent of this wickedness of yours, and pray to the Lord that, if possible, your heart's intent may be forgiven (Acts 8:18-22 CSB).

I have declared to both Jews and Greeks that they must turn to God in repentance and have faith in our Lord Jesus (Acts 20:21 NIV).

Because of your hard and unrepentant heart you are storing up wrath for yourself in the day of wrath, when God's righteous judgment is revealed. He will repay each one according to his works: eternal life to those who by persistence in doing good seek glory, honor, and mortality; but wrath and anger to those who are self-seeking and disobeyed the truth while obeying unrighteousness (Romans 2:5-8 CSB).

The following verses contain unequivocal instructions to repent, but do not suggest that failing to repent means you are not a Christian:

Jesus:

"Repent, for the kingdom of heaven has come near" (Matthew 4:17 NRSV).

After John was arrested, Jesus went to Galilee, proclaiming the good news of God: "The time is fulfilled, and the kingdom of

God has come near. Repent and believe the good news!" (Mark 1:14-15 CSB)

"I tell you, in the same way, there will be more joy in heaven over one sinner who repents than over ninety-nine righteous people who don't need repentance" (Luke 15:7 CSB).

"I tell you, in the same way, there is joy in the presence of God's angels over one sinner who repents" (Luke 15:10 CSB).

"Remember, therefore, what you have received and heard; hold it fast, and repent. But if you do not wake up, I will come like a thief, and you will not know at what time I will come to you" (Revelation 3:3 NIV).

"Those whom I love I rebuke and discipline. So be earnest and repent" (Revelation 3:19 NIV).

Disciples:

Therefore produce fruit consistent with repentance (Luke 3:8 CSB).

In the past God overlooked such ignorance, but now he commands all people everywhere to repent. For he has set the day when he will judge the world with justice by the man he has appointed (Acts 17:30-31 NIV).

I preached to those in Damascus first, and to those in Jerusalem and all the region of Judea, and to the Gentiles, that they should repent and turn to God, and do works worthy of repentance (Acts 26:19-20 CSB).

Regardless of whether repenting is essential to salvation or just something Christians should do, it is clearly a critical aspect of being a Christian. This highlights the importance of understanding the difference between regretting one's behavior and repenting of that behavior. Regret is an emotion you often experience when you wish you had behaved differently. Repentance takes regret to the next level; it involves regretting your behavior to the point of being committed to changing it.

So, as you examine whether you have become a Christian, consider whether you just regret behavior that you know is wrong, or whether you are committed to changing that behavior, even if you do so imperfectly. Regret may not get you anywhere, but repentance clearly will.

7

Must You Forgive?

As is the case with repentance, certain verses suggest that you must forgive those who wrong you to obtain God's forgiveness. Other verses instruct you to forgive those who wrong you, but do not condition God forgiving you based on you forgiving those who wrong you.

The following verses suggest that forgiving others for their wrongdoing is an integral part of obtaining God's forgiveness of your sins.

Jesus:

"For if you forgive other people when they sin against you, your heavenly Father will also forgive you. But if you do not forgive others their sins, your Father will not forgive your sins" (Matthew 6:14-15 NIV).

"And whenever you stand praying, if you have anything against anyone, forgive them, so that your Father in heaven will also forgive you your wrongdoing" (Mark 11:25 CSB). (Note: some manuscripts include verse 26: *"But if you don't forgive, neither will your Father in heaven forgive your wrongdoing."*)

The following verses contain clear instructions to forgive others, but do not appear to condition the forgiveness of your sins on you forgiving others.

"If your brother or sister sins against you, rebuke them, and if they repent, forgive them. Even if they sin against you seven times in the day, and seven times come back to you saying, 'I repent,' you must forgive them" (Luke 17:3-4 NIV).

Disciples:

And be kind and compassionate to one another, forgiving one another, just as God also forgave you in Christ (Ephesians 4:32 CSB).

Bear with one another and, if anyone has a complaint against another, forgive each other; just as the Lord has forgiven you, so you also must forgive (Colossians 3:13 NRSV).

Conclude what you will about the role forgiving others has in God's plan for your salvation. Whatever its role, it is clear that following Christ will lead you to two kinds of forgiveness: God forgiving you for the wrongs you have committed against him, and you forgiving others for the wrongs they have committed against you.

8

Must You Be One of the Elect?

No discussion of what it takes to be a Christian could be complete without addressing the elect: whether or not only those whom God chooses can become Christians. On one hand, Jesus and his followers tell us that the opportunity to become a Christian is available to all.

Jesus:

"Ask, and it will be given you; search, and you will find; knock, and the door will be opened for you. For everyone who asks receives, and everyone who searches finds, and for everyone who knocks, the door will be opened" (Matthew 7:7-8 NRSV).

Just as Moses lifted up the snake in the wilderness, so the Son of Man must be lifted up, so that everyone who believes in him may have eternal life. For God so loved the world in this way: He gave his one and only Son, so that everyone who believes in him will not perish but have eternal life. For God did not send his Son into the world to condemn the world, but to save the world through him. Anyone who believes in him is not condemned, but anyone who does not believe is already condemned, because he has not believed in the name of the one and only Son of God (John 3:14-18 CSB).

"Whoever believes in the Son has eternal life, but whoever rejects the Son will not see life, for God's wrath remains on him" (John 3:36 NIV).

"For this is the will of my Father: that everyone who sees the Son and believes in him will have eternal life, and I will raise him up on the last day" (John 6:40 CSB).

"Let anyone who is thirsty come to me and drink. Whoever believes in me, as the Scripture has said, rivers of living water will flow from within them" (John 7:37-38 NIV).

"See! I stand at the door and knock. If anyone hears my voice and opens the door, I will come into him and eat with him, and he with me" (Revelation 3:20 CSB).

"The Spirit and the bride say, 'Come!' And let him who hears say, 'Come!' Let the one who is thirsty come; and let the one who wishes take the free gift of the water of life" (Revelation 22:17 NIV).

Disciples:

Yet to all who did receive him, to those who believed in his name, he gave the right to become children of God—children born not of natural descent, nor of human decision or a husband's will, but born of God (John 1:12-13 NIV).

Then everyone who calls on the name of the Lord will be saved (Acts 2:21 CSB).

Then Peter began to speak to them: "I truly understand that God shows no partiality, but in every nation anyone who fears him and does what is right is acceptable to him" (Acts 10:34-35 NRSV).

For I am not ashamed of the gospel, because it is the power of God for salvation to everyone who believes, first to the Jew, and also to the Greek (Romans 1:16 CSB).

Christ is the culmination of the law so that there may be righteousness for everyone who believes (Romans 10:4 NIV).

For the Scripture says, Everyone who believes on him will not be put to shame, since there is no distinction between Jew and Greek, because the same Lord of all richly blesses all who call on him. For everyone who calls on the name of the Lord will be saved (Romans 10:11-13 CSB).

The Spirit and the bride say, "Come." And let everyone who hears say, "Come." And let everyone who is thirsty come. Let anyone who wishes take the water of life as a gift (Revelation 22:17 NRSV).

On the other hand, many verses in the New Testament suggest that a person only becomes a believer, and therefore a Christian, if God "draws" the person to Christ. Still other verses describe believers as the "elect" of God—ones who God chose as his own. These verses raise the difficult question of whether Christianity truly is available to anyone, or whether God makes this gift available only to certain people whom he "calls," or the "elect."

The notion that God decides whether you may become a Christian, and did so before you were even born, is unsettling. Before we review the verses that discuss this subject, let's consider the verses that provide comforting assurance that God wants, and calls, everyone to be saved.

Jesus:

"For this is the will of my Father: that everyone who sees the Son and believes in him will have eternal life, and I will raise him up on the last day" (John 6:40 CSB).

"And I, when I am lifted up from the earth, will draw all people to myself" (John 12:32 NRSV).

Disciples:

This is good, and it pleases God our Savior, who wants everyone to be saved and to come to the knowledge of the truth (1 Timothy 2:3-4 CSB).

For the grace of God has appeared, bringing salvation to all (Titus 2:11 NRSV).

The Lord does not delay his promise, as some understand delay, but is patient with you, not wanting any to perish but all to come to repentance (2 Peter 3:9 CSB).

Now, on to the rest of the "elect" verses, some of which are particularly concerning. Note that in the first of them, Jesus appears to express both ideas: that some people are chosen, but salvation is available to anyone.

Jesus:

"No one knows the Son except the Father, and no one knows the Father except the Son and anyone to whom the Son desires to reveal him. Come to me, all of you who are weary and burdened, and I will give you rest. Take up my yoke and learn from me, because I am lowly and humble in heart, and you will find rest for your souls. For my yoke is easy and my burden is light" (Matthew 11:27-30 CSB).

"For many are invited, but few are chosen" (Matthew 22:14 NIV).

"For at that time there will be great suffering, such as has not been from the beginning of the world until now, no, and never will be. And if those days had not been cut short, no one would be saved; but for the sake of the elect those days will be cut short.... For false messiahs and false prophets will appear and produce great signs and omens, to lead astray, if possible, even the elect" (Matthew 24:21-22,24 NRSV). (See also Mark 13:18-20.)

"And he will send his angels with a loud trumpet call, and they will gather his elect from the four winds, from one end of the heavens to the other" (Matthew 24:31 NIV).

"He will send out the angels and gather his elect from the four winds, from the ends of the earth to the ends of heaven" (Mark 13:27 CSB).

"And will not God grant justice to his chosen ones who cry to him day and night? Will he delay long in helping them?" (Luke 18:7 NRSV)

"For just as the Father raises the dead and gives them life, even so the Son gives life to whom he is pleased to give it" (John 5:21 NIV).

"No one can come to me unless the Father who sent me draws him, and I will raise him up at the last day" (John 6:44 CSB).

"The words I have spoken to you—they are full of the Spirit and life. Yet there are some of you who do not believe...This is why I told you that no one can come to me unless the Father has enabled them" (John 6:63,65 NIV).

Disciples:

The promise is for you and your children and for all who are far off—for all the Lord our God will call" (Acts 2:39 NIV).

When the Gentiles heard this, they rejoiced and honored the word of the Lord, and all who have been appointed to eternal life believed" (Acts 13:48 CSB).

We know that in all things God works for the good of those who love him, who have been called according to his purpose. For those God foreknew he also predestined to be conformed to the image of his Son, that he might be the firstborn among many brothers and sisters. And those he predestined he also called; those he called, he also justified; those he justified, he also glorified.... Who will bring any charge against those whom God has chosen? (Romans 8:28-30, 33 NIV)

So then, he has mercy on whom he wants to have mercy and he hardens whom he wants to harden. You will say to me, therefore, "Why then does he still find fault? For who can resist his will?" But who are you, a mere man, to talk back to God? Will what is formed say to the one who formed it, "Why did you make me like this?" Or has the potter no right over the clay, to make from the same lump one piece of pottery for honor and another for dishonor? And what if God, wanting to display his wrath and to make his power known, endured with much patience objects of wrath prepared for destruction? And what if he did this to make known the riches of his glory on objects of mercy that he prepared beforehand for glory—on us, the ones he also called, not only from the Jews but also from the Gentiles? (Romans 9:18-24 CSB)

What then? Israel did not find what it was looking for, but the elect did find it. The rest were hardened, as it is written, God gave them a spirit of stupor, eyes that cannot see and ears that cannot hear, to this day (Romans 11:7-8 CSB).

Brothers and sisters, think of what you were when you were called. Not many of you were wise by human standards; not many were influential; not many were of noble birth. But God chose the foolish things of the world to shame the wise; God chose the weak things of the world to shame the strong. God chose the lowly things of this world and the despised things—and the things that are not—to nullify the things that are, so that no one may boast before him. 30 It is because of him that you are in Christ Jesus (1 Corinthians 1:26-30 NIV).

I pray also that the eyes of your heart may be enlightened in order that you may know the hope to which he has called you (Ephesians 1:18 NIV).

Therefore I, the prisoner of the Lord, urge you to live worthy of the calling you have received (Ephesians 4:1 CSB).

He called you to this through our gospel, that you might share in the glory of our Lord Jesus Christ (2 Thessalonians 2:14 NIV).

He has saved us and called us with a holy calling, not according to our works, but according to his own purpose and grace, which was given to us in Christ Jesus before time began (2 Timothy 1:9 CSB).

Therefore I endure everything for the sake of the elect, that they too may obtain the salvation that is in Christ Jesus, with eternal glory (2 Timothy 2:10 NIV).

Paul, a servant of God and an apostle of Jesus Christ, for the faith of God's elect and their knowledge of the truth that leads to godliness (Titus 1:1 CSB).

Therefore, holy brothers and sisters, who share in the heavenly calling, fix your thoughts on Jesus, whom we acknowledge as our apostle and high priest (Hebrews 3:1 NIV).

Therefore, he is the mediator of a new covenant, so that those who are called might receive the promise of the eternal inheritance (Hebrews 9:15 CSB).

Peter, an apostle of Jesus Christ, To the exiles of the Dispersion in Pontus, Galatia, Cappadocia, Asia, and Bithynia, who have been chosen and destined by God the Father and sanctified by the Spirit to be obedient to Jesus Christ and to be sprinkled with his blood (1 Peter 1:1-2 NRSV).

So honor will come to you who believe; but for the unbelieving... They stumble because they disobeyed the word; they were destined for this. But you are a chosen race, a royal priesthood, a holy nation, a people for his possession, so that you may proclaim the praises of the one who called you out of darkness into his marvelous light (1 Peter 2:7-9 CSB).

And the God of all grace, who called you to his eternal glory in Christ, after you have suffered a little while, will himself restore you and make you strong, firm and steadfast (1 Peter 5:10 NIV).

As is the case with many topics addressed in this book, there are many articles and books on this subject. I encourage you to look into this issue as deeply as your faith requires to become comfortable with it. Taking these passages at face value, however, we must trust that Jesus calls everyone to follow him, though some may refuse the call and thereby condemn themselves to eternal life apart from God.

But if you believe that only those who God predestined to be Christians actually become Christians, are you one of those people? How can you know? That question, and how you can be sure you actually are a Christian, are really the same question. Keep reading.

9

Can You Forfeit Salvation or Become Unsavable?

You have done the things it takes to become a Christian. That's fantastic! But not so fast. To be certain you are a Christian, you also need to know:

1. Whether you can forfeit your salvation
2. Whether you can render yourself "unsavable"
3. If so, how
4. If so, whether you have done that

As it turns out, the verses that answer these questions do so inconsistently. But when Jesus or his disciples say that doing something will keep you out of heaven, you should listen.

Forfeiture

Can you forfeit your salvation after becoming a Christian? Some verses suggest the answer is yes, others no. The following verses appear to be a very straightforward way of saying, "Once a Christian, always a Christian."

God's gifts and his call are irrevocable (Romans 11:29 NIV).

For I am persuaded that neither death nor life, nor angels nor rulers, nor things present nor things to come, nor powers, nor height nor depth, nor any other created thing will be able to separate us from the love of God that is in Christ Jesus our Lord (Romans 8:38-39 CSB).

"The one who is victorious will, like them, be dressed in white. I will never blot out the name of that person from the book of life, but will acknowledge that name before my Father and his angels" (Revelation 3:5 NIV).

Other verses (some of which we covered earlier) suggest that a person may believe he or she is a Christian and be wrong. Still others suggest that a person may lose their salvation after successfully becoming a Christian.

Jesus said the following in his explanation of the Parable of the Seeds:

> *"This is the meaning of the parable: The seed is the word of God. The seed along the path are those who have heard and then devil comes and takes away the word from their hearts, so that they may not believe and be saved. And the seed on the rock are those who, when they hear, receive the word with joy. Having no root, these believe for a while and fall away in a time of testing"* (Luke 8:11-13 CSB).

This passage suggests that one can become a Christian by "receiving the word with joy" and "believing for a while" but then lose that status by "falling away" in a time of testing. This notion is also found in Paul's letter to the Hebrews:

> *It is impossible for those who have once been enlightened, who have tasted the heavenly gift, who have shared in the Holy Spirit, who have tasted the goodness of the word of God and the powers of the coming age and who have fallen away, to be brought back to repentance. To their loss they are crucifying the Son of God all over again and subjecting him to public disgrace. Land that drinks in the rain often falling on it and that produces a crop useful to those for whom it is farmed receives the blessing of God. But land that produces thorns and thistles is worthless and is in danger of being cursed. In the end it will be burned* (Hebrews 6:4-8 NIV).

James, however, anticipates that Christians will wander from the faith and be brought back.

> *Brothers and sisters, if any among you strays from the truth, and someone turns back, let that person know that whoever turns a sinner from the error of his way will save his soul from death and cover a multitude of sins* (James 5:19-20 CSB).

It isn't possible to know how many Christians have rejected their faith; most probably do not publicize this decision. But there is a recent, heartbreaking example of a lifelong Christian, a son of a pastor, doing just that. In May 2020, Jon Steingard, the lead singer of the Christian band Hawk Nelson, announced on Instagram that he no longer believes in God.[1] For Jon's sake, and the sake of others who have done the same, I hope James is right.

Many of us have doubts but don't outright reject our faith. We would like always to be sure that we believe and walk in step with God, but the human condition frequently leaves us uncertain and lacking in confidence in our faith. That's okay. It is part of the Christian journey. Don't leave your Christian journey before you arrive at your ultimate destination.

Unsavable

Next, you need to know whether doing certain things renders you ineligible for salvation. That would be a huge penalty for doing those things (what penalty could be bigger?), but there are verses that say just that.

One quote attributed to Jesus by Matthew, Mark, and Luke describes actions that, without apparent exception, would preclude a person from being forgiven. Matthew quotes Jesus as saying:

"Therefore, I tell you, people will be forgiven every sin and blasphemy, but the blasphemy against the Spirit will not be forgiven. Whoever speaks a word against the Son of Man, it will be forgiven him; but whoever speaks against the Holy Spirit, it will not be forgiven him, either in this age or the one to come" (Matthew 12:31-32 CSB).

In Mark, the quote reads:

"Truly I tell you, people will be forgiven for all sins and whatever blasphemies they utter. But whoever blasphemes against the Holy Spirit never has forgiveness, but is guilty of an eternal sin" because they were saying, *"He has an unclean spirit"* (Mark 3:28-30 CSB).

In Luke the passage states:

"And I say to you, anyone who acknowledges me before others, the Son of Man will also acknowledge him before the angels of God, but whoever denies me before others will be denied before the angels of God. Anyone who speaks a word against the Son of Man will be forgiven, but the one who blasphemes against the Holy Spirit will not be forgiven" (Luke 12:8-10 CSB).

The context of this passage in Matthew and Mark may shed some light on what blaspheming against the Holy Spirit means. Jesus made these statements after the Pharisees suggested that it was by the power of the "prince of demons" that Jesus was able to cast out demons. Matthew 12:24; Mark 3:22. Perhaps Jesus meant that a person blasphemes the Holy Spirit by attributing to Satan the power behind Jesus and his disciples' miracles. In any event, and whatever it means to do this, blaspheming against the Holy Spirit is an act that will not be forgiven; one who does this is "guilty of an eternal sin."

Assuming that being "denied before the angels of God," "not being forgiven," "never having forgiveness," and being "guilty of an eternal sin" mean not being saved, these verses describe another action that will bar a person from heaven, in addition to blaspheming against the Holy Spirit: denying Jesus before others. The quoted language does not say that this penalty is limited to non-Christians; it is unqualified. The following verse is similarly clear about the implications of denying Jesus:

No one who denies the Son has the Father; everyone who confesses the Son has the Father also (1 John 2:23 NRSV).

How may these verses be reconciled with those that describe belief in Jesus as the exclusive means of salvation? Perhaps a person who truly believes in Jesus could not, or would not, deny Jesus or blaspheme against the Holy Spirit. But then what do we make of Peter, who Jesus called the rock on which he would build his church, but then denied Jesus three times? (See Matthew 16:18, 26:69-75.) If you decide to look into this further, you will find no shortage of opinions on the matter.

Whatever the answer, these verses should dissuade all who regard themselves as Christians from denying Jesus or blaspheming the Holy Spirit. You do not want to find out after it is too late that you disqualified yourself from being saved by doing these things.

In addition to the above verses, Jesus tells us that we will not enter the kingdom of heaven unless we do something other than believe in him: he says that we must achieve a certain level of "righteousness":

> *"For I tell you, unless your righteousness exceeds that of the scribes and Pharisees, you will never enter the kingdom of heaven"* (Matthew 5:20 NRSV).

This is troubling in a number of ways, not the least of which is: Who in the world knows how to measure your righteousness against the righteousness of the Pharisees? It is of some comfort that, given the way Jesus rebuked this group throughout his ministry, the bar appears to be low. But still, in this quote, Jesus conditions our ability to enter the kingdom of heaven on a certain level of righteousness, even though he also makes clear that good works cannot earn our salvation.

Given the uncertainty these verses create, you would be well advised to stay clear of any words or actions that put you in jeopardy of either forfeiting your salvation or rendering yourself unsavable. But these verses highlight the central inquiry of this book: What relationship does your behavior have to your status as a Christian?

That's what the rest of this book is about.

PART II:

ARE YOU SURE?

Now you know what it takes to become a Christian and, I assume, you have done those things. But how can you be sure that what you did actually made you a Christian?

First, you need to understand what Jesus and his disciples said is the test for whether you actually are a Christian. This part of the book inventories and organizes the verses in which Jesus and his disciples explain the test, what questions are on it, and what the correct answers are. Read them.

Then, take the test.

10

Conduct Matters

The passages quoted in Part I make it clear that having faith that Jesus is God's son and accepting him as your Savior are essential to becoming a Christian. But how can you be sure that you are a Christian, i.e. that your faith and your manner of accepting Jesus did the trick? What role does your behavior play in your assuredness that you are a Christian? Can you believe in Jesus and accept him as your Savior, live an unrepentant, sinful life, and still expect salvation, forgiveness, or a place in heaven? In other words, if you claim to be a Christian, but don't behave like one, did you ever really become a Christian?

Earlier, we covered the important point that doing good things does not make you a Christian. A corresponding and equally important point is the one made in the following verses: that if you truly are a Christian, your "rebirth" as a Christian will manifest itself in your conduct. For example, although being generous does not make you a Christian, passages we will cover later say that, if you are a Christian, you should be generous. Likewise, although remaining faithful to your spouse does not make you a Christian, if you are a Christian, you should be faithful to your spouse. The bottom line: When you are looking for certainty that you are a Christian, your conduct matters.

> *"Not everyone who says to me, 'Lord, Lord,' will enter the kingdom of heaven, but only the one who does the will of my Father in heaven. On that day many will say to me, 'Lord, Lord, didn't we prophecy in your name, drive out demons in your name, and do many miracles in your name? Then I will announce to them, 'I never knew you. Depart from me, you lawbreakers!'"*
> (Matthew 7:21-23 CSB)

"Everyone then who hears these words of mine and acts on them will be like a wise man who built his house on rock. The rain fell, the floods came, and the winds blew and beat on that house, but it did not fall, because it had been founded on rock. And everyone who hears these words of mine and does not act on them will be like a foolish man who built his house on sand. The rain fell, and the floods came, and the winds blew and beat against that house, and it fell—and great was its fall!" (Matthew 7:24-27 NRSV)

"Why do you call me 'Lord, Lord,' and don't do the things I say? I will show you what someone is like who comes to me, hears my words, and acts on them: He is like a man building a house, who dug deep and laid the foundation on the rock. When the flood came, the river crashed against that house and couldn't shake it, because it was well built. But the one who hears and does not act is like a man who built the house on the ground without a foundation. The river crashed against it, and immediately it collapsed. And the destruction of that house was great" (Luke 6:46-49 CSB).

"My mother and brothers are those who hear God's word and put it into practice" (Luke 8:21 NIV).

But he said, "Blessed rather are those who hear the word of God and obey it!" (Luke 11:28 NRSV)

"If anyone serves me, he must follow me. Where I am, there my servant also will be. If anyone serves me, the Father will honor him" (John 12:26 CSB).

We are witnesses to these things, and so is the Holy Spirit, whom God has given to those who obey him (Acts 5:32 NIV).

For we are God's handiwork, created in Christ Jesus to do good works, which God prepared in advance for us to do (Ephesians 2:10 NIV).

"Look, I am coming soon, and my reward is with me to repay

each person according to his work. I am the Alpha and the Omega, the first and the last, the beginning and the end. Blessed are those who wash their robes, so that they may have the right to the tree of life and may enter the city by the gates. Outside are the dogs, the sorcerers, the sexually immoral, the murderers, the idolaters, and everyone who loves and practices falsehood" (Revelation 22:12-15 CSB).

In the passage from Matthew 7 quoted on page 58, Jesus tells us that it is not enough to call Jesus "Lord" to enter the kingdom of heaven. Entry into the kingdom is only for "he who does the will of" God. This suggests action—the doing of certain things. But what things?

The above verse from Ephesians tells us that Christians are created to do "good works," works that God prepared in advance for us to do. This suggests that God's plan for your life as a Christian includes doing things that are part of his greater plan. But what things? And if God has given you a part to play in his plan, how can you fail to play that part?

The verses on this subject make up a continuum, or a spectrum. At one end of the spectrum, certain verses tell us that, in keeping with the idea that faith in Jesus alone is the source of salvation, your conduct is not related to your salvation. At the other, various passages state that your behavior is inextricably linked to your salvation. Still others fall in the middle, suggesting that certain behavior is expected of Christians but without linking behavior and salvation.

Jesus spoke of his own obedience to God, and the importance of Christians' obedience to his teachings, in no uncertain terms:

"So that the world may know that I love the Father, I do as the Father commanded me.... If you keep my commands you will remain in my love, just as I have kept my Father's commands and remain in his love" (John 14:31; 15:10 CSB).

Jesus also said:

"Be perfect, therefore, as your heavenly Father is perfect" (Matthew 5:48 NIV).

When giving his disciples the Great Commission, Jesus told them to spread his teachings all over the world:

"...baptizing them in the name of the Father and of the Son and of the Holy Spirit, teaching them to observe everything I have commanded you (Matthew 28:19-20 CSB).

In these verses and those quoted earlier in this chapter, Jesus communicated the importance of obeying his instructions, phrasing it as an imperative. That is reason enough to do as he said. But given your desire to be certain of your status as a Christian, you will want to explore other verses that provide more information about the role of conduct in the spiritual life of a Christian, and what your behavior says about whether you are, in fact, a Christian. We will get to those verses shortly.

The verses that describe belief in Jesus, through the grace of God, as the source of salvation are clear. Just as clear, however, are verses that describe how behavior relates to one's status as a Christian. Though a person cannot achieve salvation without believing in Jesus and accepting him as Savior, many passages of scripture state that if you engage in certain types of conduct, you are not going to have eternal life.

Some of these verses are virtually "if-then" statements: if you do this, then you won't go to heaven; if you do that, then you will. Other verses suggest that, if one behaves in a certain way, that person is a Christian; if one behaves in other ways, one cannot actually be a Christian, because a true believer simply would not behave that way. These verses provide a framework by which you may examine whether you are a Christian in a tangible way: by comparing your behavior to the standards they set.

Among the most telling of the verses that discuss the relationship of behavior to salvation are those that insist that believers "change." They describe the consequences of failing to change in no uncertain terms. They highlight the distinction between knowledge of Christ and his teachings, and acceptance of Christ as Lord and Savior, with corresponding obedience to his teachings. The most well-informed person may know all about Christ and the New Testament, but if they do not accept Christ, become a Christian, and put their beliefs into action through obedience to Christ's instructions, this knowledge is purely academic and insufficient to achieve salvation. As James puts it: "You believe that God is one. Good! Even the demons believe— and they shudder" (James 2:19 CSB).

Jesus:

"Truly I tell you, unless you change and become like children, you will never enter the kingdom of heaven. Whoever becomes humble like this child is the greatest in the kingdom of heaven" (Matthew 18:3-4 NRSV).

Disciples:

And those who belong to Christ Jesus have crucified the flesh with its passions and desires (Galatians 5:24 NRSV).

You were taught, with regard to your former way of life, to put off your old self, which is being corrupted by its deceitful desires; to be made new in the attitude of your minds; and to put on the new self, created to be like God in true righteousness and holiness (Ephesians 4:22-24 NIV).

For if we deliberately go on sinning after receiving the knowledge of the truth, there no longer remains a sacrifice for sins, but a terrifying expectation of judgment and the fury of a fire about to consume the adversaries. Anyone who disregarded the law of Moses died without mercy, based on the testimony of two or three witnesses. How much worse punishment do you think one will deserve who has trampled on the Son of God, who has disregarded as profane the blood of the covenant by which he was sanctified, and who has insulted the Spirit of grace? (Hebrews 10:26-29 CSB)

A number of passages describe behavior in relation to attaining salvation or eternal life without reference to belief in Jesus. While these verses do not negate, and can be read in harmony with, those that speak of belief in Jesus is the source of salvation, we must also account for their clear implications about the role of behavior in God's plan of salvation.

Just then a man came to Jesus and asked, "Teacher, what good thing must I do to get eternal life?" "Why do you ask me about what is good?" Jesus replied. "There is only One who is good. If you want to enter life, keep the commandments." "Which ones?" he inquired. Jesus replied, "'You shall not murder, you shall not commit adultery, you shall not steal, you shall not give false testimony, honor your father and mother,' and 'love your neighbor as yourself.'" "All these I have kept," the young man said. "What do I still lack?" Jesus answered, "If you want to be perfect, go, sell your possessions and give to the poor, and you will have treasure in heaven. Then come, follow me." When the young man heard this, he went away sad, because he had great wealth. Then Jesus said to his disciples, "Truly I tell you, it is hard for someone who is rich to enter the kingdom of heaven" (Matthew 19:16-23 NIV). See also Mark 10:17-23, Luke 18:18-25.

If actions were not connected to salvation, this passage would not make sense. This man asked Jesus a question about the relationship of actions to "getting eternal life": what good thing must I do? He did not ask what he must believe, and Jesus did not tell him what he must believe. Jesus told him that, to "enter life," he must keep the commandments, and then listed those that Jesus regarded as essential.

Compare that passage to the following passage, in which a similar question drew a different response from Jesus, one that focuses on belief:

"Don't work for the food that perishes but for the food that lasts for eternal life, which the Son of Man will give you, because God the Father has set his seal of approval on him." "What can we do

to perform the works of God?" they asked him. Jesus replied, "This is the work of God—that you believe in the one he has sent" (John 6:27-29 CSB).

In this passage, people asked Jesus what they can "do to perform the works of God." Rather than answering as he did to the rich young man that they should follow the commandments, Jesus told them that the work of God is to believe in Jesus.

At the end of the story of the rich young man, Jesus remarked on how difficult it will be for a rich person to enter the kingdom of heaven—after the rich man was saddened by the prospect of selling his possessions and giving the money to the poor "to be perfect." If all it takes to enter heaven is to believe in Jesus, why would it be more difficult for a rich person to do this than a poor person, and why would Jesus make this remark only after the rich man became sad at the prospect of selling his possessions?

In the following passage, Jesus offers guidance about attaining salvation that combines beliefs and actions: To inherit eternal life, one must "love."

Then an expert in the law stood up to test him, saying, "Teacher, what must I do to inherit eternal life?" "What is written in the law?" he asked him. "How do you read it?" He answered, "Love the Lord your God with all your heart, with all your soul, with all your strength, and with all your mind," and "your neighbor as yourself." "You've answered correctly," he told him. "Do this and you will live" (Luke 10:25-28 CSB).

Similar verses appear elsewhere in the New Testament and include a warning that misbehavior will preclude a person from inheriting the kingdom of God.

Now the works of the flesh are obvious: fornication, impurity, licentiousness, idolatry, sorcery, enmities, strife, jealousy, anger, quarrels, dissensions, factions, envy, drunkenness, carousing, and things like these. I am warning you, as I warned you before: those who do such things will not inherit the kingdom of God (Galatians 5:19-21 NRSV).

Do not love the world or the things in the world. If anyone loves the world, the love of the Father is not in him. For everything in the world—the lust of the flesh, the lust of the eyes, and the pride in one's possessions—is not from the Father but is from the world (1 John 2:15-16 CSB).

Perhaps the most dramatic image that illustrates the scriptural link between behavior and salvation is the picture Jesus paints of Judgment Day.

"When the Son of Man comes in his glory, and all the angels with him, he will sit on his glorious throne. All nations will be gathered before him, and he will separate the people one from another as a shepherd separates the sheep from the goats. He will put the sheep on his right and the goats on his left. Then the King will say to those on his right, 'Come, you who are blessed by my Father; take your inheritance, the kingdom prepared for you since the creation of the world. For I was hungry and you gave me something to eat, I was thirsty and you gave me something to drink, I was a stranger and you invited me in, I needed clothes and you clothed me, I was sick and you looked after me, I was in prison and you came to visit me.' Then the righteous will answer him, 'Lord, when did we see you hungry and feed you, or thirsty and give you something to drink? When did we see you a stranger and invite you in, or needing clothes and clothe you? When did we see you sick or in prison and go to visit you?' The King will reply, 'Truly I tell you, whatever you did for one of the least of these brothers and sisters of mine, you did for me.' Then he will say to those on his left, 'Depart from me, you who are cursed, into the eternal fire prepared for the devil and his angels. For I was hungry and you gave me nothing to eat, I was thirsty and you gave me nothing to drink, I was a stranger and you did not invite me in, I needed clothes and you did not clothe me, I was sick and in prison and you did not look after me.' They also will answer, 'Lord, when did we see you hungry or thirsty or a stranger or needing clothes or sick or in prison, and did not help you?' He will reply, 'Truly I tell you, whatever you did not do for

one of the least of these, you did not do for me.' Then they will go away into eternal punishment, but the righteous to eternal life" (Matthew 25:31-46 NIV).

As in the rich man story, Jesus could have explained that, on Judgment Day, souls will be sorted into those who believed, and are therefore saved, and those who didn't, and are therefore damned. But he did not do that. Instead, he described the attributes of those who are blessed and will inherit the kingdom of heaven exclusively with reference to their actions: they gave; they invited; they clothed; they looked after; they visited. He did the same with respect to the shortcomings of the souls he will send to hell: they gave nothing; they did not invite; they did not clothe; they did not look after.

If behavior has no bearing on one's status as a Christian, why would Jesus place such emphasis on behavior when describing the most dramatic, gut-wrenching moment all of us will ever experience—standing before God and learning whether we will enter heaven or be cast into hell? In these verses, Jesus tells us what questions are on the test we are taking while we are alive, what the correct answers are, and how he will grade us after we die. There is no reason to believe he got the questions or the answers wrong. And the questions and answers are all about our behavior—the outward manifestations of what we truly believe. The next chapter explains in more detail, through more verses, what questions are on the test and how, as a Christian, you should be answering them through your conduct.

11

The Test

Let's say you describe yourself as a child care professional. You believe the most important thing a person can do in life is provide children with a loving, nurturing environment. Through study and education, you equip yourself to become the best child care professional there is. You sincerely commit yourself to a life of doing nothing but caring for children. You proudly proclaim yourself a child care professional for the rest of your days.

But what if you never actually care for a single child? Instead, you counsel couples about the virtue of not having children and the hardships associated with having them. You do your best to prevent children from being born, and you are good at your job. Were you ever really a child care professional?

Turning back to the point of this book: Can you be a Christian but not practice Christianity? Should calling yourself a Christian, and sincerely believing you are one, give you comfort that you are a Christian if you don't do what Christians should do, and do things that Christians should not do?

When I started the project that later became this book, I set out to answer those very questions by identifying standards against which I could test myself to determine whether I truly am a Christian. It turns out that the test is not that hard to find. Jesus spelled it out for us himself:

"Very truly I tell you, whoever believes in me will do the works I have been doing. He will do even greater things than these... If you love me, keep my commands...Whoever has my commands and keeps them is the one who loves me. The one who loves me will be loved by my Father, and I too will love them and show myself to them.... Anyone who loves me will obey my teaching. My Father will love them, and we will come to them and make

our home with them. Anyone who does not love me will not obey my teaching" (John 14:12, 15, 21, 23, 24 NIV).

"If you keep my commands you will remain in my love, just as I have kept my Father's commands and remain in his love. I have told you these things so that my joy may be in you and your joy may be complete" (John 15:10-11 CSB).

It is difficult to find a clearer explanation for how people may test themselves to determine whether they are truly Christians. How do you know if you believe in Jesus? "Whoever believes in me will do the works I have been doing." How do you know if you love Jesus? "If you love me, keep my commands... Whoever has my commands and keeps them is the one who loves me.... Anyone who loves me will obey my teaching. Anyone who does not love me will not obey my teaching." How do you know if you remain in his love? "If you keep my commands you will remain in my love."

Jesus' disciples said exactly the same thing:

Therefore, brothers and sisters, we have an obligation—but it is not to the flesh, to live according to it. For if you live according to the flesh, you will die; but if by the Spirit you put to death the misdeeds of the body, you will live. For those who are led by the Spirit of God are the children of God (Romans 8:12-14 NIV).

He will punish those who do not know God and do not obey the Gospels of our Lord Jesus (2 Thessalonians 1:8 NIV).

This is how we know that we know him: if we keep his commands. The one who says, "I have come to know him," and yet doesn't keep his commands, is a liar, and the truth is not in him. But whoever keeps his word, truly in him the love of God is made complete. This is how we know we are in him: The one who says he remains in him should walk just as he walked (1 John 2:3-6 CSB).

If anyone has material possessions and sees a brother or sister in need but has no pity on them, how can the love of God be in that person? Dear children, let us not love with words or speech but with actions and in truth. This is how we know that we belong to the truth and how we set our hearts at rest in his presence: If our hearts condemn us, we know that God is greater than our hearts, and he knows everything. Dear friends, if our hearts do not condemn us, we have confidence before God and receive from him anything we ask, because we keep his commands and do what pleases him. And this is his command: to believe in the name of his Son, Jesus Christ, and to love one another as he commanded us. The one who keeps God's commands lives in him, and he in them. And this is how we know that he lives in us: We know it by the Spirit he gave us (1 John 3:17-24 NIV).

And there it is. If you believe in Jesus and accept him as your Savior, you will do what Jesus told you to do; you will "walk just as he walked." The more you do that, the more confidence you may have that you are a Christian. The less you do it, the less confident you will be. And if you do not obey Jesus' commands at all, and instead live with a sinful nature, according to many verses you will be punished and "die."

But how are you, as a Christian, supposed to live, specifically? Fortunately, the Bible gives us plenty of information on that score. The New Testament is filled with Jesus' instructions about how his followers are to behave. Some are direct quotes from him, others his followers' paraphrase of his teachings. Jesus' teachings about how Christians are to conduct themselves are inseparable from his instructions about the belief, faith, and repentance that produce salvation. Christians who wish to measure their conduct against Jesus' commands will not want for sources of comparison.

Less clear is the answer to a rather interesting, if academic, question that these verses raise: Do Christians behave well because they choose to or because their new nature as Christians causes them to? There are verses that support both conclusions.

Certain verses suggest that Christians choose to behave in a Christ-like manner and that Christ-like behavior is the product of a conscious decision to behave that way. Others suggest that, when one becomes a Christian, Christ-like behavior flows from the presence of

the Holy Spirit dwelling inside the Christian and that Christ-like behavior is an effect of Christianity, or a marker of one who has become a Christian.

Reasonable people may disagree about whether these concepts
are mutually exclusive. Perhaps it's a little bit of both: that accepting
Christ and the indwelling of the Holy Spirit inspire and compel us to
behave as Jesus did. In any event, these concepts and the verses that
discuss them also highlight a question that all Christians struggle
with: If I chronically misbehave, am I truly a Christian? I hope the
rest of this book will help you answer that question.

Christian Behavior Is a Choice

The following verses regard good behavior as the product of a
conscious choice to behave as Jesus taught. They say that Christians
should choose certain behavior and explain why they do it. Providing
reasons is an effort to persuade; persuasion is only necessary if the
one being persuaded is free to make a choice. Reasons to behave well
would not matter to someone who is under compulsion or has no say
in the matter. Likewise, if merely being a Christian caused a person to
live without sin, no encouragement to live a sinless life would be necessary; you just would do it. These verses, however, suggest that
Christians make a conscious choice to behave as Jesus taught them to.

*In the same way, count yourselves dead to sin but alive to God in
Christ Jesus. Therefore do not let sin reign in your mortal body
so that you obey its evil desires. Do not offer the parts of your
body to sin as instruments of wickedness, but rather offer yourselves to God as those who have been brought from death to life;
and offer every part of yourself to him as instruments for righteousness. For sin shall no longer be your master, because you
are not under the law, but under grace* (Romans 6:11-14 NIV).

*For those who live according to the flesh have their minds set on
the things of the flesh, but those who live according to the Spirit
have their minds set on the things of the Spirit. Now the mind-set
of the flesh is death, but the mind-set of the Spirit is life and*

peace. The mind-set of the flesh is hostile to God because it does not submit to God's law. Indeed, it is unable to do so. Those who are in the flesh cannot please God. You, however, are not in the flesh, but in the Spirit, if indeed the Spirit of God lives in you (Romans 8:5-9 CSB).

Therefore I urge you, brothers and sisters, in view of God's mercy, to offer your bodies as a living sacrifice, holy and pleasing to God—this is your true and proper worship. Do not conform to the pattern of this world, but be transformed by the renewing of your mind. Then you will be able to test and approve what God's will is—his good, pleasing and perfect will (Romans 12:1-2 NIV).

Therefore I, the prisoner of the Lord, urge you to live worthy of the calling you have received, with all humility and gentleness, with patience, bearing with one another in love, making every effort to keep the unity of the Spirit through the bond of peace (Ephesians 4:1-3 CSB).

You were taught, with regard to your former way of life, to put off your old self, which is being corrupted by its deceitful desires; 23 to be made new in the attitude of your minds; and to put on the new self, created to be like God in true righteousness and holiness (Ephesians 4:22-24 NIV).

For you were once darkness, but now you are light in the Lord. Live as children of light—for the fruit of the light consists of all goodness, righteousness, and truth—testing what is pleasing to the Lord. Don't participate in the fruitless works of darkness, but instead expose them (Ephesians 5:8-11 CSB).

For God did not call us to be impure, but to live a holy life. Therefore, anyone who rejects this instruction does not reject a human being but God, the very God who gives you his Holy Spirit (1 Thessalonians 4:7-8 NIV).

Christian Behavior Is an Effect

Other verses describe or treat Christians' good behavior as a product or outpouring of their relationship with Jesus, rather than a choice they make. They suggest that good behavior is an effect of being a Christian and a way of identifying one. Many verses written by the disciples speak of Christ-like behavior as an immutable characteristic of a Christian, who is "controlled by the Spirit," who is a "new creation," and whose obedience "comes from faith." Paul asks, "We died to sin; how can we live in it any longer?" In 1 John this idea is expressed even more forcefully: "He is not able to sin, because he has been born of God" (1 John 3:9 CSB).

Jesus:

"By this everyone will know that you are my disciples, if you love one another" (John 13:35 NIV).

"Likewise, every good tree bears good fruit, but a bad tree bears bad fruit. A good tree cannot bear bad fruit, and a bad tree cannot bear good fruit. Every tree that does not bear good fruit is cut down and thrown into the fire. Thus, by their fruit you will recognize them" (Matthew 7:17-20 NIV).

"For the mouth speaks from the overflow of the heart. A good person produces good things from his storeroom of good, and an evil person produces evil things from his storeroom of evil" (Matthew 12:34-35 CSB).

"Everyone who does evil hates the light, and will not come into the light for fear that their deeds will be exposed. But whoever lives by the truth comes into the light, so that it may be seen plainly that what they have done has been done in the sight of God" (John 3:20-21 NIV).

Disciples:

Therefore, if anyone is in Christ, he is a new creation; the old has passed away, and see, the new has come! (2 Corinthians 5:17 CSB)

Through him we received grace and apostleship to call all the Gentiles to the obedience that comes from faith for his name's sake (Romans 1:5 NIV).

What should we say then? Should we continue in sin so that grace may multiply? Absolutely not! How can we who died to sin still live in it? (Romans 6:1-2 CSB)

For we know that our old self was crucified with him so that the body ruled by sin might be done away with, that we should no longer be slaves to sin—because anyone who has died has been set free from sin (Romans 6:6-7 NIV).

Don't you know that if you offer yourselves to someone as obedient slaves, you are slaves of that one you obey—either of sin leading to death or of obedience leading to righteousness? But thank God that, although you used to be slaves of sin, you obey from the heart that pattern of teaching to which you were handed over, and having been set free from sin, you became enslaved to righteousness. I am using a human analogy because of the weakness of your flesh. For just as you offered the parts of yourselves as slaves to impurity, and to greater and greater lawlessness, so now offer them as slaves to righteousness, which results in sanctification (Romans 6:16-19 CSB).

But now that you have been set free from sin and have become slaves of God, the benefit you reap leads to holiness, and the result is eternal life (Romans 6:22 NIV).

For we are his workmanship, created in Christ Jesus for good works, which God prepared ahead of time for us to do (Ephesians 2:10 CSB).

Therefore, my dear friends, as you have always obeyed—not only in my presence, but now much more in my absence—continue to work out your salvation with fear and trembling, for it is God who works in you to will and to act in order to fulfill his good purpose (Philippians 2:12-13 NIV).

What good is it, my brothers and sisters, if someone claims to have faith but has no deeds? Can such faith save them? Suppose a brother or a sister is without clothes and daily food. If one of you says to them, "Go in peace; keep warm and well fed," but does nothing about their physical needs, what good is it? In the same way, faith by itself, if it is not accompanied by action, is dead (James 2:14-17 NIV).

You believe that God is one. Good! Even the demons believe— and they shudder. Senseless person! Are you willing to learn that faith without works is useless? Wasn't Abraham our father justified by works in offering Isaac his son on the altar? You see that faith was active together with his works, and by works, faith was made complete, and the Scripture was fulfilled that says, Abraham believed God, and it was credited to him as righteousness, and he was called God's friend. You see that a person is justified by works and not by faith alone. In the same way, wasn't Rahab the prostitute also justified by works in receiving the messengers and sending them out by a different route? For just as the body without the Spirit is dead, so also faith without works is dead (James 2:19-26 CSB).

God is light; in him there is no darkness at all. If we claim to have fellowship with him and yet walk in the darkness, we lie and do not live out the truth. But if we walk in the light, as he is in the light, we have fellowship with one another, and the blood of Jesus, his Son, purifies us from all sin (1 John 1:5-7 NIV).

The one who says he is in the light but hates his brother or sister is in the darkness until now. The one who loves his brother or sister remains in the light, and there is no cause for stumbling in him. But the one who hates his brother or sister is in the darkness, walks in the darkness, and doesn't know where he's going, because the darkness has blinded his eyes (1 John: 2:9-11 CSB).

No one who lives in him keeps on sinning. No one who continues to sin has either seen him or known him (1 John 3:6 NIV).

Children, let no one deceive you. The one who does what is right is righteous, just as he is righteous. The one who commits sin is of the devil, for the devil has sinned from the beginning. The Son of God was revealed for this purpose: to destroy the devil's works. Everyone who has been born of God does not sin, because his seed remains in him; he is not able to sin, because he has been born of God. This is how God's children and the devil's children become obvious. Whoever does not do what is right is not of God, especially the one who does not love his brother or sister (1 John 3:7-10 CSB).

Those who say, "I love God," and hate their brothers or sisters, are liars; for those who do not love a brother or sister whom they have seen, cannot love God whom they have not seen. The commandment we have from him is this: those who love God must love their brothers and sisters also (1 John 4:20-21 NRSV).

Everyone who believes that Jesus is the Christ has been born of God, and everyone who loves the Father also loves the one born of him. This is how we know that we love God's children: when we love God and obey his commands. For this is what love for God is: to keep his commands (1 John 5:1-3 CSB).

We knew that anyone born of God does not continue to sin; the One who was born of God keeps them safe, and the evil one cannot harm them (1 John 5:18 NIV).

Anyone who does not remain in Christ's teaching and goes beyond it does not have God. The one who remains in that teaching, this one has both the Father and the Son (2 John 1:9 CSB).

Dear friend, do not imitate what is evil but what is good. Anyone who does what is good is from God. Anyone who does what is evil has not seen God (3 John 1:11 NIV).

Some of these verses seem to say that Christians do not sin, and therefore, if you continue to sin you are not a Christian. But certainly some of us must be Christians, even though all of us continue to sin. You must wrestle with these verses, along with all of the other verses quoted in this book that deal with how you can be confident you are a Christian even though you continue to sin because you are imperfect.

Other Verses Linking Christian Behavior and Salvation

But wait, there's more. Many other passages in the New Testament address the relationship of good behavior and salvation, and bad behavior and damnation. Add these to the list of the verses you must account for as you test your status as a Christian against Jesus and his disciples' teachings. They reinforce the idea that, while good works will not save you, if you really are saved, your beliefs will manifest themselves in good works. On the other hand, if you keep ending up in the wrong place behavior-wise, you are probably not on the right path.

Jesus:

"For whoever does the will of my Father in heaven is my brother and sister and mother" (Matthew 12:50 CSB). See also Mark 3:30, Luke 8:21.

"For truly I tell you, whoever gives you a cup of water to drink because you bear the name of Christ will by no means lose the reward" (Mark 9:41 NRSV).

"Therefore produce fruit consistent with repentance... The ax is already at the root of the trees. Therefore, every tree that doesn't produce good fruit will be cut down and thrown into the fire." "What then should we do?" the crowds were asking him. He replied to them, "The one who has two shirts must share with someone who has none, and the one who has food must do the same" (Luke 3:8-11 CSB).

"Do not judge, and you will not be judged. Do not condemn, and you will not be condemned. Forgive, and you will be forgiven; give, and it will be given to you... for the measure you give will be the measure you get back" (Luke 6:37-38 NRSV).

"For whoever is ashamed of me and my words, the Son of Man will be ashamed of him when he comes in his glory and that of the Father and the holy angels" (Luke 9:26 CSB).

"Sell your possessions and give to the poor. Provide purses for yourselves that will not wear out, a treasure in heaven that will never fail, where no thief comes near and no moth destroys. For where your treasure is, there your heart will be also" (Luke 12:33-34 NIV).

"Do not be amazed at this, because the time is coming when all who are in the graves will hear his voice and come out—those who have done good things, to the resurrection of life, but those who have done wicked things, to the resurrection of condemnation" (John 5:28-29 CSB).

Disciples:

I truly understand that God shows no partiality, but in every nation anyone who fears him and does what is right is acceptable to him (Acts 10:34-35 NRSV).

And he died for all so that those who live should no longer live for themselves, but for the one who died for them and was raised (2 Corinthians 5:15 CSB).

But because of your stubbornness and your unrepentant heart, you are storing up wrath against yourself for the day of God's wrath, when his righteous judgment will be revealed. God "will repay each person according to what they have done." To those who by persistence in doing good seek glory, honor and immortality, he will give eternal life. But for those who are self-seeking and who reject the truth and follow evil, there will be wrath and anger. There will be trouble and distress for every human being who does evil: first for the Jew, then for the Gentile; but glory, honor and peace for everyone who does good: first for the Jew, then for the Gentile. For God does not show favoritism (Romans 2:5-11 NIV).

All who sin without the law will also perish without the law, and all who sin under the law will be judged by the law. For the hearers of the law are not righteous before God, but the doers of the law will be justified (Romans 2:12-13 CSB).

But now that you have been set free from sin and have become slaves to God, the benefit you reap leads to holiness, and the result is eternal life (Romans 6:22 NIV).

For in Christ Jesus neither circumcision nor on circumcision accomplishes anything; what matters is faith working through love (Galatians 5:6 CSB).

Do not be deceived: God cannot be mocked. A man reaps what he sows. Whoever sows to please their flesh, from the flesh will reap destruction; whoever sows to please the Spirit, from the Spirit will reap eternal life. Let us not become weary in doing good, for at the proper time we will reap a harvest if we do not give up. Therefore, as we have opportunity, let us do good to all people, especially to those who belong to the family of believers (Galatians 6:7-10 NIV).

For know and recognize this: Every sexually immoral or impure or greedy person, who is an idolater, does not have an inheritance in the kingdom of Christ and of God (Ephesians 5:5 CSB).

Do not lie to each other, since you have taken off your old self with its practices and have put on a new self, which is being renewed in knowledge in the image of its Creator (Colossians 3:9-10 NIV).

Whatever you do, do it from the heart, as something done for the Lord and not for people, knowing that you will receive the reward of an inheritance from the Lord. You serve the Lord Christ.

For the wrongdoer will be payback for whatever wrong he is done, and there is no favoritism (Colossians 3:23-25 CSB).

"The Lord knows those who are his," and, "Everyone who confesses the name of the Lord must turn away from wickedness" (2 Timothy 2:19 NIV).

If we say, "We have fellowship with him," and yet we walk in darkness, we are lying and are not practicing the truth. If we walk in the light as he himself is in the light, we have fellowship with one another, and the blood of Jesus his Son cleanses us from all sin (1 John 1:6-7 CSB).

Recap

This is a good place to summarize what we've learned so far. You need to do certain things to have confidence that you are a Christian. First, you must believe in Jesus: that he is the Son of God, sent here to die for the forgiveness of sin for those who believe and follow him. Second, you must accept him, and ask him to be your Lord and Savior. Third, you should repent and forgive others, and you may need to be among the Elect. Fourth, your faith should manifest itself in conduct that is appropriate for a Christian.

Though you cannot become a Christian by doing good things or living a good life, if you are a Christian, your faith will cause you, by choice or compulsion, to live according to Christ's teachings. You will not live a life characterized by a pattern of sin. Instead, you will continually strive to live as Jesus and his disciples said you should and repent from sinful behavior, having been inspired or compelled by the Holy Spirit to behave in a manner pleasing to God. The test of whether you are a Christian is whether your conduct manifests a sincere, genuine, heart-felt faith in Christ.

12

Judgment Day

Before we get to the specific ways God expects Christians to behave, let's look at their significance in another context. We have been addressing the implications of our conduct with respect to whether we are, or are not, Christians. But even assuming that we are Christians, what are the implications of our behavior when we stand before God and he judges us? Can we look at ourselves through the lens God does, with knowledge of how our actions today will impact our eternal lives tomorrow even if we are saved? As it turns out, and as we touched on earlier: yes, we can. And the view is bracing.

Some Christians are under the impression that, because they are saved, they have a "get out of jail free" card; they do not need to worry about their misbehavior because their sins are forgiven. It is not that simple.

For example, consider the manner in which Paul addresses this subject in a single chapter of Hebrews. First:

The Holy Spirit also testifies to us about this. First he says: "This is the covenant I will make with them after that time, says the Lord. I will put my laws in their hearts, and I will write them on their minds." Then he adds: "Their sins and lawless acts I will remember no more." And where these have been forgiven, sacrifice for sin is no longer necessary (Hebrews 10:15-18 NIV).

But just a few verses later, Paul states:

For if we deliberately go on sinning after receiving the knowledge of the truth, there no longer remains a sacrifice for sins, but a terrifying expectation of judgment and the fury of a fire about to consume the adversaries (Hebrews 10:26-27 CSB).

These are not words of comfort to those who deliberately keep sinning after becoming Christians. They are words of warning.

Someday, we all will stand before God and give an account of ourselves. God's promise that we are saved allows us to expect to spend eternity in heaven. His promise does not mean, however, that we will not hear about our behavior when we get there. Jesus and his disciples encourage us to conduct ourselves as if the Rapture is imminent, and with good reason.

Jesus:

"But about that day or hour no one knows, neither the angels in heaven, nor the Son, but only the Father. Beware, keep alert; for you do not know when the time will come. It is like a man going on a journey, when he leaves home and puts his slaves in charge, each with his work, and commands the doorkeeper to be on the watch. Therefore, keep awake—for you do not know when the master of the house will come, in the evening, or at midnight, or at cockcrow, or at dawn, or else he may find you asleep when he comes suddenly. And what I say to you I say to all: Keep awake" (Mark 13:32-37 NRSV).

"You also be ready, because the Son of Man is coming at an hour you do not expect" (Luke 12:40 CSB).

"Be on guard so that your hearts are not weighed down with dissipation and drunkenness and the worries of this life, and that day does not catch you unexpectedly, like a trap. For it will come upon all who live on the face of the whole earth. Be alert at all times, praying that you may have the strength to escape all these things that will take place, and to stand before the Son of Man" (Luke 21:34-36 NRSV).

Disciples:

I have a hope in God, which these men themselves also accept, that there will be a resurrection, both of the righteous and the unrighteous. I always strive to have a clear conscience toward God and men (Acts 24:15-16 CSB).

The night is nearly over; the day is almost here. So let us put aside the deeds of darkness and put on the armor of light (Romans 13:12 NIV).

So now, little children, remain in him so that when he appears we may have confidence and not be ashamed before him at his coming (1 John 2:28 CSB).

But the day of the Lord will come like a thief. The heavens will disappear with a roar; the elements will be destroyed by fire, and the earth and everything done in it will be laid bare. Since everything will be destroyed in this way, what kind of people ought you to be? You ought to live holy and godly lives as you look forward to the day of God and speed its coming. That day will bring about the destruction of the heavens by fire, and the elements will melt in the heat. But in keeping with his promise we are looking forward to a new heaven and a new earth, where righteousness dwells. So then, dear friends, since you are looking forward to this, make every effort to be found spotless, blameless and at peace with him (2 Peter 3:10-14 NIV).

These verses make it clear that our conduct has eternal implications even though we are Christians. As the following verses illustrate more vividly, God is going to put you on trial. He will sit as judge without a jury. Unlike ordinary trials, where the person on trial presents evidence, God will already have all the evidence: He will already know everything you have ever thought, said, and done. He will put this evidence on full display to everyone, with no lawyerly spin. And, unlike our legal system, there will be no appeal, no time waiting for your sentence to be carried out, and no chance for parole. God will deliver your punishment or reward immediately and permanently.

You can't do anything about the aspects of your life that already are in evidence. But you can make sure that the evidence that comes in from this point forward is replete with behavior that manifests a sincere faith in Jesus and a commitment to following his teachings.

On that Day Everything Will Be Laid Bare

Do you have a secret that you hope no one will ever learn? Good luck with that. Jesus promises us that all of our misdeeds will be laid before everyone, and before God himself, on Judgment Day.

"For there is nothing hidden that will not be disclosed, and nothing concealed that will not be known or brought out into the open" (Luke 8:17 NIV).

"There is nothing covered that will be uncovered, nothing hidden that won't be made known. Therefore, whatever you have said in the dark will be heard in the light, and what you have whispered in any year in private rooms will be proclaimed on the house tops" (Luke 12:2-3 CSB).

Paul used this idea when explaining why people should not judge others. Although we have imperfect information here on earth, we will all have perfect information in heaven. This will allow everyone to understand why God judges each person as he will.

Therefore judge nothing before the appointed time; wait till the Lord comes. He will bring to light what is hidden in darkness and will expose the motives of the heart. At that time each will receive his praise from God (1 Corinthians 4:5 NIV).

Even before that day, God is aware of all that we do, good and bad. Isn't that reason enough to behave the way he expects?

No creature is hidden from him, but all things are naked and exposed to the eyes of him to whom we must give an account (Hebrews 4:13 CSB).

The sins of some are obvious, reaching the place of judgment ahead of them; the sins of others trail behind them. In the same way, good deeds are obvious, and even those that are not obvious cannot remain hidden forever (1 Timothy 5:24-25 NIV).

All Will Face God's Judgment

Our deeds, secrets, and motives having been made known to all, God will dispense justice to everyone, both those who are to be saved and those who are to be condemned.

Jesus:

"I tell you that on the day of judgment people will have to account for every careless word they speak. For by your words you will be acquitted, and by your words you will be condemned" (Matthew 12:36-37 CSB).

"Do not judge, and you will not be judged; do not condemn, and you will not be condemned. Forgive, and you will be forgiven; give, and it will be given to you. ... for the measure you give will be the measure you get back" (Luke 6:37-38 NRSV).

Disciples:

Therefore, having overlooked the times of ignorance, God now commands all people everywhere to repent, because he has set the day when he is going to judge the world in righteousness by the man he has appointed (Acts 17:30-31 CSB).

But because of your stubbornness and your unrepentant heart, you are storing up wrath against yourself for the day of God's wrath, when his righteous judgment will be revealed (Romans 2:5 NIV).

But you, why do you judge your brother or sister? Or you, why do you despise your brother or sister? For we will all stand before the judgment seat of God. For it is written, As I live, says the Lord, every knee will bow to me, and every tongue will give praise to God. So then, each of us will give an account of himself to God. Therefore, let us no longer judge one another. Instead decide never to put a stumbling block or pitfall in the way of your brother or sister (Romans 14:10-13 CSB).

Everyone Will Be Punished or Rewarded for What They Have Done

How may we reconcile verses in the Bible that speak of forgiveness of sins with those that, like these, make it clear that each of us will have to answer for our conduct before God? Reading these verses together and consistently, one is left with the inescapable conclusion that forgiveness does not mean complete freedom from accountability for our behavior. Instead, on Judgment Day, even if we are forgiven and will ultimately find ourselves in heaven, we will have to "give an account" of ourselves, literally in front of God and everybody. Then, we will get our due, whatever God may deem that to be, given the way we behaved ourselves on earth. (Although we reviewed some of these verses in previous chapters, they bear repeating here.)

Jesus:

"For the Son of Man is going to come with in his Father's glory with his angels, and then he will reward each person according to what they have done" (Matthew 16:27 NIV).

"When the Son of Man comes in his glory, and all the angels with him, then he will sit on his glorious throne. All nations will be gathered before him, and he will separate them one from another, just as a shepherd separates the sheep from the goats. He will put the sheep on his right and the goats on the left. Then the King will say to those on his right, 'Come, you who are blessed by my Father: inherit the kingdom prepared for you from the foundation of the world. For I was hungry and you gave me something to eat; I was thirsty and you gave me something to drink; I was a stranger and you took me in; I was naked and you clothed me; I was sick and you took care of me; I was in prison and you visited me.' Then the righteous will answer him, 'Lord, when did we see you hungry and feed you, or thirsty and give you something to drink? When did we see you a stranger and take it and, or without clothes and clothe you? When did we see you

sick, or in prison, and visit you?' And the King will answer them, 'Truly I tell you, whatever you did for one of the least of these brothers and sisters of mine, you did for me.' Then he will also say to those on the left, 'Depart from me, you who are cursed, into the eternal fire prepared for the devil and his angels! For I was hungry and you gave me nothing to eat; I was thirsty and you gave me nothing to drink; I was a stranger and you didn't take me in; I was naked and you didn't clothe me, sick and in prison and you didn't take care of me.' Then they too will answer, 'Lord when did we see you hungry, or thirsty, or a stranger, or without clothes, or sick, or in prison, and not help you?' Then he will answer them, 'Truly I tell you, whatever you did not do for one of the least of these, you did not do for me.' And they will go away into eternal punishment, but the righteous into eternal life" (Matthew 25:31-46 CSB).

"Do not be amazed at this, for a time is coming when all who are in their graves will hear his voice and come out—those who have done what is good will rise to live, and those who have done what is evil will rise to be condemned" (John 5:28-29 NIV).

"Look, I am coming soon, and my reward is with me to repay each person according to his work" (Revelation 22:12 CSB).

Disciples:

Because of your hard and unrepentant heart you are storing up wrath for yourself in the day of wrath, when God's righteous judgment is revealed. He will repay each one according to his works: eternal life to those who by persistence in doing good seek glory, honor, and immortality; but wrath and anger to those who are self-seeking and disobeyed the truth while obeying unrighteousness. There will be affliction and distress for every human being who does evil, first to the Jew, and also to the Greek; but glory, honor, and peace for everyone who does what is good, first to the Jew, and also to the Greek. For there is no favoritism with God (Romans 2:5-11 CSB).

Now if anyone builds on the foundation with gold, silver, precious stones, wood, hay, straw— the work of each builder will become visible, for the Day will disclose it, because it will be revealed with fire, and the fire will test what sort of work each has done. If what has been built on the foundation survives, the builder will receive a reward. If the work is burned up, the builder will suffer loss; the builder will be saved, but only as through fire (1 Corinthians 3:12-15 NRSV).

For we must all appear before the judgment seat of Christ, so that each may be repaid for what he has done in the body, whether good or evil (2 Corinthians 5:10 CSB).

Do not be deceived: God cannot be mocked. A man reaps what he sows. Whoever sows to please their flesh, from the flesh will reap destruction; whoever sows to please the Spirit, from the Spirit will reap eternal life. Let us not become weary in doing good, for at the proper time we will reap a harvest if we do not give up. Therefore, as we have opportunity, let us do good to all people, especially to those who belong to the family of believers (Galatians 6:7-10 NIV).

Whatever you do, do it from the heart, as something done for the Lord and not for people, knowing that you will receive the reward of an inheritance from the Lord. You serve the Lord Christ. For the wrongdoer will be paid back for whatever wrong he is done, and there is no favoritism (Colossians 3:23-25 CSB).

He will punish those who do not know God and do not obey the gospel of our Lord Jesus. They will be punished with everlasting destruction and shut out from the presence of the Lord and from the glory of his might on the day he comes to be glorified in his holy people and to be marveled at among all those who have believed (2 Thessalonians 1:8-10 NIV).

I also saw the dead, the great and the small, standing before the throne, and books were opened. Another book was opened, which is the book of life, and the dead were judged according to their works by what was written in the books. Then the sea gave up the dead that were in it, and death and Hades gave up the dead that were in them; each one was judged according to their works. Death and Hades were thrown into the lake of fire. This is the second death, the lake of fire. And anyone whose name was not found written in the book of life was thrown into the lake of fire (Revelation 20:12-15 CSB).

In light of these verses, we can be sure that God will judge everyone, the saved and unsaved alike, for how we conduct ourselves on earth. He will distribute rewards and punishments accordingly, while we are living and after we die. We want the rewards, and definitely do not want the punishments, regardless of what they are. But, just out of curiosity, what do those rewards and punishments look like?

13

Rewards for the Saved

Jesus and his disciples spoke rather vaguely about the rewards our conduct in this life will earn us. Some passages describe these rewards in a relative manner, being more or less than those others will receive. Other verses describe rewards that are act-specific: If you do certain things, you will receive a certain reward.

Will Christians receive their rewards on earth, or must they wait until they enter heaven? Some verses describe a heavenly reward, others an earthly reward, and some are unclear whether the reward is heavenly or earthly. But, for purposes of this book, the most important thing about these verses is that they address Christians being rewarded in heaven based on what they do, not what they believe.

These verses are encouraging when viewed from the perspective of a person concerned about the impact of their behavior on their status as a Christian. These passages recognize that, even among Christians, some people behave better and others worse; some even go so far as to break commandments. But they teach us that, provided you are saved, the consequences of your bad behavior—even breaking some of the commandments—is a limited reward, not the absence of salvation. The benefit of good behavior is a greater reward in heaven.

So, in these verses you may find some comfort that God's plan of salvation allows for some degree of non-compliance with Jesus' teachings. Other verses we have already considered, however, make it equally clear that there is a limit on how far a person who is truly a Christian will depart from those teachings. Wherever that line is, these verses make clear that your actions have eternal significance even if you are saved.

Jesus:

"Therefore, whoever breaks one of the least of these command-ments, and teaches others to do the same, will be called least in the kingdom of heaven; but whoever does them and teaches them will be called great in the kingdom of heaven" (Matthew 5:19 NRSV).

"But when you give to the poor, don't let your left hand know what your right hand is doing, so that your giving may be in se-cret. And your Father who sees in secret will reward you" (Matthew 6:3-5 CSB).

"Whoever welcomes you welcomes me, and whoever welcomes me welcomes the one who sent me. Whoever welcomes a prophet in the name of a prophet will receive a prophet's reward; and whoever welcomes a righteous person in the name of a righteous person will receive the reward of the righteous; and whoever gives even a cup of cold water to one of these little ones in the name of a disciple—truly I tell you, none of these will lose their reward" (Matthew 10:40-42 NRSV).

"And everyone who has left houses or brothers or sisters or fa-ther or mother or wife or children or fields for my sake will re-ceive a hundred times as much and will inherit eternal life. But many who are first will be last, and many who are last will be first" (Matthew 19:29-30 NIV).

"Truly I tell you," Jesus said, *"there is no one who has left house or brothers or sisters or mother or father or children or fields for my sake and for the sake of the gospel, who will not receive a hundred times more, now at this time—houses, brothers and sis-ters, mothers and children, and fields, with persecutions—and eternal life in the age to come. But many who are first will be last, and the last first"* (Mark 10:29-31 CSB). See also Luke 18:29.

"But love your enemies, do what is good, and lend, expecting nothing in return. Then your reward will be great, and you will

be children of the Most High" (Luke 6:35 CSB).

"But when you give a banquet, invite the poor, the crippled, the lame, the blind, and you will be blessed. Although they cannot repay you, you will be repaid at the resurrection of the righteous" (Luke 14:13-14 NIV).

"So if I, your Lord and Teacher, have washed your feet, you also ought to wash one another's feet. For I have given you an example, that you also should do just as I have done for you. Truly I tell you, a servant is not greater than his master, and a messenger is not greater than the one who sent him. If you know these things, you are blessed if you do them" (John 13:14-17 CSB).

Disciples:

Serve wholeheartedly, as if you were serving the Lord, not people, because you know that the Lord will reward each one for whatever good they do, whether they are slave or free (Ephesians 6:7-8 NIV).

Whatever you do, do it from the heart, as something done for the Lord, not for people, knowing that you will receive the reward of an inheritance from the Lord. For the wrongdoer will be paid back for whatever wrong he has done, and there is no favoritism (Colossians 3:23-25 CSB).

So much for the rewards. What about the punishments?

14

Punishment for the Condemned

In contrast to the large or small heavenly reward that awaits those who are saved, incomprehensible punishment awaits those who are not. Many of the verses that describe this punishment make its nature perfectly understandable. It will be like being thrown into an all-consuming fire. What is incomprehensible is its duration. Who can imagine being on fire forever? But the New Testament tells us that this is the fate of those who are not Christians. It is also interesting to note that, like many of the verses regarding rewards, the verses regarding punishment link the degree of punishment to behavior, not a failure to believe.

Jesus:

"The ax is already at the root of the trees, and every tree that does not produce good fruit will be cut down and thrown into the fire" (Matthew 3:10 NIV).

"Therefore, just as the weeds are gathered and burned in the fire, so it will be at the end of the age. The Son of Man send out his angels, and they will gather from his kingdom all who cause sin and those guilty of lawlessness. They will throw them into the blazing furnaces where there will be weeping and gnashing of teeth" (Matthew 13:40-42 CSB).

"So it will be at the end of the age. The angels will come out and separate the evil from the righteous and throw them into the furnace of fire, where there will be weeping and gnashing of teeth" (Matthew 13:49-50 NRSV).

"If any of you put a stumbling block before one of these little ones who believe in me, it would be better for you if a great mill-

stone were fastened around your neck and you were drowned in the depth of the sea" (Matthew 18:6 NRSV).

[At the conclusion of the parable of the unforgiving servant] *"And because he was angry, his master handed him over to the jailers to be tortured until he could repay everything that was owned. So also my heavenly father will do to you unless every one of you forgives his brother or sister from your heart"* (Matthew 18:34-35 CSB).

[At the conclusion of the parable about a master and a misbehaving servant] *"The master of that servant will come on a day when he does not expect him and at an hour he is not aware of. He will cut him to pieces and assign him a place with the hypocrites, where there will be weeping and gnashing of teeth"* (Matthew 24:50-51 NIV).

"And if your hand causes you to fall away, cut it off. It is better for you to enter life maimed than to have two hands and go to hell, the unquenchable fire. And if your foot causes you to fall away, cut it off. It is better for you to enter life lame than to have two feet and to be thrown into hell. And if your eye causes you to fall away, gouge it out. It is better for you to enter the kingdom of God with one eye than to have two eyes and be thrown into hell, where their worm does not die, and the fire is not quenched" (Mark 9:43-48 CSB).

"I am the vine, you are the branches. Those who abide in me and I in them bear much fruit, because apart from me you can do nothing. Whoever does not abide in me is thrown away like a branch and withers; such branches are gathered, thrown into the fire, and burned" (John 15:5-6 NRSV).

"But the cowards, faithless, detestable, murderers, sexually immoral, sorcerers, idolaters, and all liars—their share will be in the lake that burns with fire and sulfur, which is the second death" (Revelation 21:8 CSB).

Disciples:

Speak and act as those who are to be judged by the law of freedom. For judgment is without mercy to the one who has not shown mercy. Mercy triumphs over judgment (James 2:12-13 CSB).

The Lord knows how to rescue the godly from trials and to hold the unrighteous for punishment on the day of judgment. This is especially true of those who follow the corrupt desire of the flesh and despise authority (2 Peter 2:9-10 NIV).

But these people, like irrational animals—creatures of instinct born to be caught and destroyed—slander what they do not understand, and in their destruction they too will be destroyed. They will be paid back with harm for the harm they have done (2 Peter 2:12-13 CSB).

And anyone whose name was not found written in the book of life was thrown into the lake of fire (Revelation 20:15 NRSV).

Wow. Eternally swimming in a lake of fire. Being tortured forever, not to mention living forever without God's love, which would be bad enough all by itself.

Perhaps, even after all that, you need more reasons to behave well. The next chapter inventories those reasons, understanding that no reasons could be as compelling as those you just read. Then we will turn to how Jesus and his disciples said Christians should, and should not, behave.

15

Other Reasons To Behave

In light of what lies in store on Judgment Day, you should not need more reasons to behave in keeping with Christ's instructions. But if you do, it just so happens that there quite a number of others. Jesus and his disciples give us some insight about the importance of Christians' behavior in God's plan of salvation. They help us answer the question, "Why should Christians behave well, other than 'Jesus said so'?"

You will please God.

"Be perfect, therefore, as your heavenly Father is perfect" (Matthew 5:48 NIV).

...so that we may lead a tranquil and quiet life in all godliness and dignity. This is good, and it pleases God our Savior, who wants everyone to be saved and to come to the knowledge of the truth (1 Timothy 22-3 CSB).

Do your best to present yourself to God as one approved, a worker who does not need to be ashamed and who correctly handles the word of truth (2 Timothy 2:15 NIV).

But as the one who called you is holy, you also are to be holy in all your conduct; for it is written, Be holy, because I am holy (1 Peter 1:15-16 CSB).

Since we have these promises, dear friends, let us purify ourselves from everything that contaminates body and spirit, perfecting holiness out of reverence to God (2 Corinthians 7:1 NIV).

You will be with God.

Finally brothers and sisters, whatever is true, whatever is honorable, whatever is just, whatever is pure, whatever is lovely, whatever is commendable—if there is any moral excellence and if there is anything praiseworthy—dwell on these things. Do what you have learned and received and heard from me, and seen in me, and the God of peace will be with you (Philippians 4:8-9 CSB).

You will be a more effective witness.

"You are the light of the world. A city built on a hill cannot be hid. No one after lighting a lamp puts it under the bushel basket, but on the lampstand, and it gives light to all in the house. In the same way, let your light shine before others, so that they may see your good works and give glory to your Father in heaven" (Matthew 5:14-16 NRSV).

We are not giving anyone an occasion for offense, so that the ministry not be blamed. Instead, as God's ministers, we commend ourselves in everything (2 Corinthians 6:3-4 CSB).

Live such good lives among the pagans that, though they accuse you of doing wrong, they may see your good deeds and glorify God on the day he visits us (1 Peter 2:12 NIV).

You will inspire other Christians.

Because of the proof provided by this ministry, they will glorify God for your obedient confession of the gospel of Christ, and for your generosity in sharing with them and with everyone. And as they pray on your behalf, they will have deep affection for you because of the surpassing grace of God in you (2 Corinthians 9:13-14 CSB).

You will set an example for children.

"But if anyone causes one of these little ones—those who believe

in me—to stumble, it would be better for them to have a large millstone hung around their neck and to be drowned in the depths of the sea" (Matthew 18:6 NIV). See also Mark 9:42; Luke 17:1-3.

In the same way, encourage the young men to be self-controlled in everything. Make yourself an example of good works with integrity and dignity in your teaching (Titus 2:6-7 CSB).

You will avoid causing others to sin.

He said to his disciples, "Offenses will certainly come, but woe to the one through whom they come! It would be better for him if a millstone were hung around his neck and he were thrown into the sea than for him to cause one of these little ones to stumble" (Luke 17:1-2 CSB).

[B]ut it is wrong for you to make others fall by what you eat; it is good not to eat meat or drink wine or do anything that makes your brother or sister stumble (Romans 14:20-21 NRSV).

But be careful that this right of yours in no way becomes a stumbling block to the weak. For if someone sees you, the one who has knowledge, dining in an idol's temple, won't his weak conscience be encouraged to eat food offered to idols? So the weak person, the brother or sister for whom Christ died, is ruined by your knowledge. Now when you sin like this against brothers and sisters and wound their weak conscience, you are sinning against Christ. Therefore, if food causes my brother or sister to fall, I will never again eat meat, so that I won't cause my brother or sister to fall (1 Corinthians 8:9-13 CSB).

Do not cause anyone to stumble (1 Corinthians 10:32 NIV).

You will avoid sinning by omission.

So it is sin to know the good and yet not do it (James 4:17 CSB).

You will make your love, joy, and belief complete.

As the Father has loved me, so have I loved you. Now remain in my love. If you obey my commands, you will remain in my love, just as I obeyed my Father's commands and remain in his love. I have told you this so that my joy may be in you and that your joy may be complete (John 15:9-11 NIV).

Therefore, my dear brothers and sisters, be steadfast, immovable, always excelling in the Lord's work, because you know that your labor in the word is not in vain (1 Corinthians 15:58 CSB).

You see that [Abraham's] faith and his actions were working together, and his faith was made complete by what he did... You see that a person is considered righteous by what they do and not by faith alone (James 2:22-24 NIV).

God is love, and the one who remains in love remains in God, and God remains in him. In this, love is made complete with us so that we may have confidence in the day of judgment, because as he is, so also are we in this world (1 John 4:16-17 CSB).

Therefore, rid yourselves of all malice, deceit, hypocrisy, envy, and slander of every kind. Like newborn babies, crave pure spiritual milk, so that by it you may grow up in your salvation, now that you have tasted that the Lord is good (1 Peter 2:1-3 NIV).

You will treat your body like the temple it is.

Flee sexual immorality! Every other sin a person commits is outside the body, but the person who is sexually immoral sins against his own body. Don't you know that your body is a temple of the Holy Spirit who is in you, whom you have from God? You are not your own, you were bought at a price. So glorify God with your body (1 Corinthians 6:18-20 CSB).

You will improve the lives of others.

For it is God's will that by doing good you should silence the ignorant talk of foolish people (1 Peter 2:15 NIV).

Do not fear what they fear or be intimidated, but in your hearts regard Christ the Lord as holy, ready at any time to give a defense to anyone who asks you for a reason for the hope that is in you. Yet do this with gentleness and respect, keeping a clear conscience, so that when you are accused, those who disparage your good conduct in Christ will be put to shame (1 Peter 3:14-16 CSB).

You will demonstrate wisdom and understanding.

Who is wise and understanding among you? Let them show it by their good life, by deeds done in the humility that comes from wisdom (James 3:13 NIV).

I can almost hear you saying, "I get it, I need to be on good behavior. Enough already." Mission accomplished. Now on to the verses that tell you how to go about doing that.

16

What God Expects: The Big Picture

The verses we have reviewed so far make it clear that your actions play an important role in your status as a Christian. They play an important role in God's plan of salvation for you and for those with whom you interact.

But what, exactly, does God expect of you? The New Testament is filled with verses that describe the behavior that God expects of Christians. The following verses paint the big picture. We will get to the details shortly.

Disciples:

Live in harmony with one another (Romans 12:16 NIV).

If possible, as far as it depends on you, live at peace with everyone (Romans 12:18 CSB).

Let us therefore make every effort to do what leads to peace and to mutual edification (Romans 14:19 NIV).

Each one of us is to please his neighbor for his good, to build him up (Romans 15:2 CSB).

Accept one another, then, just as Christ accepted you, in order to bring praise to God (Romans 15:7 NIV).

Be alert, stand firm in the faith, be courageous, be strong. Do everything in love (1 Corinthians 16:13-14 CSB).

For he chose us in him before the creation of the world to be holy and blameless in his sight (Ephesians 1:4 NIV).

Do everything without grumbling and arguing, so that you may be blameless and pure, children of God who are faultless in a crooked and perverted generation, among whom you shine like stars in the world, by holding firm to the word of life (Philippians 2:14-16 CSB).

Let your gentleness be evident to all (Philippians 4:5 NIV).

Finally brothers and sisters, whatever is true, whatever is honorable, whatever is just, whatever is pure, whatever is lovely, whatever is commendable—if there is any moral excellence and if there is anything praiseworthy—dwell on these things. Do what you have learned and received and heard from me, and seen in me, and the God of peace will be with you (Philippians 4:8-9 CSB).

...so that you may live a life worthy of the Lord and please him in every way: bearing fruit in every good work, growing in the knowledge of God, being strengthened with all power according to his glorious might so that you may have great endurance and patience, and giving joyful thanks to the Father, who has qualified you to share in the inheritance of his holy people in the kingdom of light (Colossians 1:10-12 NIV).

Since, then, you have been raised with Christ, set your hearts on things above, where Christ is, seated at the right hand of God. Set your mind on things above, not on earthly things (Colossians 3:1-2 NIV).

Finally, be strengthened by the Lord and by his vast strength. Put on the full armor of God so that you can stand against the schemes of the devil. For our struggle is not against flesh and blood, but against the rulers, against the authorities, against the cosmic powers of this darkness, against evil, spiritual forces in the heavens. For this reason take up the full armor of God, so that you may be able to resist the evil day, and having prepared everything to take your stand. Stand, therefore, with truth like a belt around your waist, righteousness like armor on your chest, and your feet sandaled with readiness for the gospel of peace. In every situation take up the shield of faith with which you can ex-

tinguish all the flaming arrows of the evil one. Take the helmet of salvation and the sword of the Spirit—which is the word of God. Pray at all times in the Spirit with every prayer and request, and stay alert with all perseverance and intercession for all the saints (Ephesians 6:10-18 CSB).

Therefore encourage one another and build each other up as you are already doing (1 Thessalonians 5:11 CSB).

Live in peace with each other. And we urge you, brothers and sisters, warn those who are idle and disruptive, encourage the disheartened, help the weak, be patient with everyone. Make sure that nobody pays back wrong for wrong, but always strive to do what is good for each other and for everyone else (1 Thessalonians 5:13-15 NIV).

Do not rebuke an older man harshly, but exhort him as if he were your father. Treat younger men as brothers, older women as mothers, and younger women as sisters, with absolute purity. Give proper recognition to those widows who are really in need (1 Timothy 5:1-3 NIV).

Flee from youthful passions, and pursue righteousness, faith, love, and peace, along with those who call on the Lord from a pure heart. But reject foolish and ignorant disputes, because you know that they breed quarrels (2 Timothy 2:22-23 CSB).

For the grace of God has appeared, bringing salvation for all people, instructing us to deny godlessness and worldly lusts and to live a sensible, righteous, and godly way in the present age (Titus 2:11-12 CSB).

But the wisdom that comes from heaven is first of all pure; then peace-loving, considerate, submissive, full of mercy and good fruit, impartial and sincere. Peacemakers who sow in peace raise a harvest of righteousness (James 3:17-18 NIV).

Therefore, rid yourselves of all malice, all deceit, hypocrisy, envy, and all slander. Like newborn infants, desire the pure milk of the word, so that you may grow up into your salvation, if you have tasted that the Lord is good (1 Peter 2:1-3 CSB).

For this very reason, make every effort to supplement your faith with goodness, goodness with knowledge, knowledge with self-control, self-control with endurance, endurance with godliness, godliness with brotherly affection, and brotherly affection with love. For if you possess these qualities in increasing measure, they will keep you from being useless or unfruitful in the knowledge of our Lord Jesus Christ. The person who lacks these things is blind and shortsighted and has forgotten the cleansing from his past sins (2 Peter 1:5-9 CSB).

So that's the big picture. What are the specifics? The next two chapters inventory the New Testament's Christian dos and don'ts. They also include current, extra-biblical information about these behaviors to create context that may help you apply the verses to your life.

Some of that information consists of statistics and stories about how other people engage in a certain behavior or not. This information will help you evaluate your behavior in relation to others. But don't forget that how other people behave is not the issue. The benchmark against which you ultimately must measure your behavior is not how other people behave, but how Jesus behaved and instructed you to behave.

Other information included in the next two chapters addresses how engaging in, and not engaging in, some of these behaviors is actually good for you and will improve your life and the lives of others. I hope this information will help you see that living your life the way Jesus instructs is not an exercise in hardship and sacrifice. It is an exercise in self-improvement, which also allows your beliefs as a Christian to manifest themselves and improve your Christian resume. Those are good reasons to engage in (or avoid, as the case may be) those behaviors. But the ultimate reason you should engage in or avoid those behaviors is that, as a Christian, you are motivated by love, which, in turn, should prompt you to embrace certain behaviors and flee from others.

Finally, as you read the dos and don'ts, also keep in mind the reason they are part of this book: to help you determine whether the evidence of your faith, as manifested in your behavior, gives you confidence that you are a Christian. As someone once asked, "If being a Christian was a crime, would there be enough evidence to convict you?" Given what will happen on Judgment Day, which we covered in Chapter 12, the more important question is: "If getting into heaven depends on whether your behavior reflects a sincere faith in Jesus, will God find enough evidence to admit you?"

Read the dos and don'ts closely, as though you are studying for a test. You are.

17

Christian Dos

LOVE AND SERVE GOD

Loving and serving God is what being a Christian is all about, isn't it? Good for you for wanting to do this. We need as many people to join that effort as we can get.

The number of people who even believe in the Christian God, much less love and serve him, is falling. While 90 percent of Americans believe in a higher power, only 56 percent believe in God as the Bible describes him.[2] That means a third of Americans believe in some other "higher power." That's an awful lot of people when one considers that only about half believe in the Christian God.

Worshipping and praising God in church are common ways of loving and serving him. So, it is concerning that, even among Christians, the number attending church is falling. According to Gallup, between 1962 and 2019 (roughly my lifetime so far), the percentage of people surveyed who stated their religious preference was Protestant fell by half; from 69 percent to 35 percent.[3] During the same period, the percentage of people who said they have "no religion" rose from 2 percent (2 percent!) to 21 percent, while the percentage who identified as Catholics stayed essentially the same; it fell from 24 percent to 22 percent.[4]

Another Gallup poll revealed that only 50 percent of Americans belonged to a church, synagogue, or mosque in 2018; that number was down from 76 percent in the 1940's, but as recently as the late 1990's the number was 70 percent.[5] Just 42 percent of millennials are members of churches.[6] While attending church is not the only way people can demonstrate their love for and desire to serve God, it is one of them. And clearly the trend among Americans is away from attending church.

Jesus:

He said to him, "Love the Lord your God with all your heart, with all your soul, and with all your mind. This is the greatest and most important command" (Matthew 22:37-38 CSB).

"It is written, 'Worship the Lord your God, and serve only him'" (Luke 4:8 NRSV).

Disciples:

Do not lack diligence in zeal; be fervent in the Spirit; serve the Lord (Romans 12:11 CSB).

Always give yourselves fully to the work of the Lord, because you know that your labor in the Lord is not in vain (1 Corinthians 15:58 NIV).

LOVE OTHERS

Love is a special emotion, one that we naturally reserve for a select group of people. To love others indiscriminately is asking a lot.

Often the most effective way to feel something that you don't is to behave as if you did and let the feeling follow. For example, if you are not happy at the moment, act as if you are and you will start feeling happy.

The same is true of loving others. You may not feel love for a stranger or a neighbor you don't know particularly well. But if you start doing things for them that are in keeping with loving them, the feeling will follow.

Jesus:

"Love your neighbor as yourself" (Matthew 19:19 CSB). See also Matthew 22:39; Luke 10:27-28.

"I give you a new command: Love one another. Just as I have loved you, you are also to love one another. By this everyone will know that you are my disciples, if you love one another" (John 13:34-35 CSB).

"This is my commandment, that you love one another as I have loved you" (John 15:12 NRSV).

Disciples:

Let love be without hypocrisy. Detest evil; cling to what is good. Love one another deeply as brothers and sisters. Outdo one another in showing honor (Romans 12:9-10 CSB).

Let no debt remain outstanding, except the continuing debt to love one another, for whoever loves others has fulfilled the law. The commandments, "You shall not commit adultery," "You shall not murder," "You shall not steal," "You shall not covet," and whatever other command there may be, are summed up in this one command: "Love your neighbor as yourself" (Romans 13:8-10 NIV).

If I speak human or angelic tongues that do not have love, I am a noisy gong or a clanging symbol. If I have the gift of prophecy and understand all mysteries and all knowledge, and if I have all faith so that I can move mountains but do not have love, I am nothing. And if I give away all my possessions, and if I give over my body in order to boast but do not have love, I gain nothing (1 Corinthians 13:1-3 CSB).

Follow the way of love and eagerly desire gifts of the spirit (1 Corinthians 14:1 NIV).

For you were called to be free, brothers and sisters; only don't use this freedom as an opportunity for the flesh, but serve one another through love. For the whole law is fulfilled in one statement: Love your neighbor as yourself (Galatians 5:13-14 CSB).

But the fruit of the Spirit is love, joy, peace, forbearance, kindness, goodness, faithfulness, gentleness and self-control. Against such things there is no law (Galatians 5:22-23 NIV).

Therefore I, the prisoner of the Lord, urge you to live worthy of the calling you have received, with all humility and gentleness, with patience, bearing with one another in love, making every effort to keep the unity of the Spirit through the bond of peace (Ephesians 4:1-3 CSB).

Follow God's example, therefore, as dearly loved children and walk in the way of love, just as Christ loved us (Ephesians 5:1-2 NIV).

If then there is an encouragement in Christ, if any consolation of love, if any fellowship with the Spirit, if any affection and mercy, make my joy complete by thinking the same way, having the same love, united in spirit, intent on one purpose (Philippians 2:1-2 CSB).

Now concerning love of the brothers and sisters, you do not need to have anyone write to you, for you yourselves have been taught by God to love one another (1 Thessalonians 4:9 NRSV).

Let brotherly love continue. Don't neglect to show hospitality, for by doing this some have welcomed angels as guests without knowing it (Hebrews 13: 1-2 CSB).

If you really keep the royal law found in Scripture, "Love your neighbor as yourself," you are doing right (James 2:8 NIV).

Since you have purified yourselves by your obedience to the truth, so that you show sincere brotherly love for each other, from a pure heart love one another constantly, because you have been born again (1 Peter 1:22-23 CSB).

Show proper respect to everyone, love the family of believers, fear God, honor the emperor (1 Peter 2:17 NIV).

Finally, all of you be like-minded and sympathetic, love one another, and be compassionate and humble (1 Peter 3:8 CSB).

Above all, love each other deeply, because love covers over a multitude of sins (1 Peter 4:8 NIV).

For this is the message you have heard from the beginning: We should love one another (1 John 3:11 CSB).

We know that we have passed from death to life because we love our brothers and sisters. The one who does not love remains in death. Everyone who hates his brother or sister is a murderer, and you know that no murderer has eternal life residing in him. This is how we have come to know love: He laid down his life for us. We should also lay down our lives for our brothers and sisters (1 John 3:14-16 CSB).

Dear friends, let us love one another, for love comes from God. Everyone who loves has been born of God and knows God. Whoever does not love does not know God, because God is love (1 John 4:7-8 NIV).

If we love one another, God remains in us and his love is made complete in us (1 John 4:12 CSB).

Those who say, "I love God," and hate their brothers or sisters, are liars; for those who do not love a brother or sister whom they have seen, cannot love God whom they have not seen. The commandment we have from him is this: those who love God must love their brothers and sisters also (1 John 4:20-21 NRSV).

So now I ask you, dear lady—not as if I were writing you a new command, but one we have had from the beginning—that we love one another. This is love: that we walk according to his commands. This is the command as you have heard it from the beginning: that you walk in love (2 John 1:5-6 CSB).

FOLLOW THE GOLDEN RULE

A simple rule that, if universally followed, would make the world a delightful place: Treat others as you want to be treated. Norman Rockwell determined that the Golden Rule is common to all religions.[7] Other sources confirm that some form of the Golden Rule is part of all major religions and non-religious ethical systems.[8] It is certainly central to Jesus' teachings.

Jesus:

"So in everything, do to others what you would have them do to you, for this sums up the Law and Prophets" (Matthew 7:12 NIV).

"Do unto others as you would have them do to you" (Luke 6:31 NRSV).

BE HOLY

Dictionary.com defines "holy" as "dedicated or consecrated to God or a religious purpose." If you can't honestly say that you are dedicated or consecrated to God, that is easily remedied: Dedicate yourself to him. If you are not dedicated to a religious purpose, pick one and dedicate yourself to it.

Disciples:

Since we have these promises, dear friends, let us purify ourselves from everything that contaminates body and spirit, perfecting holiness out of reverence for God (2 Corinthians 7:1 NIV).

For God has not called us to impurity but to live in holiness. Consequently, anyone who rejects this does not reject man, but God, who gives you his Holy Spirit (1 Thessalonians 4:7-8 CSB).

...that we may live peaceful and quiet lives in all godliness and holiness. This is good, and pleases God our Savior (1 Timothy 2:2-3 NIV).

Pursue peace with everyone, and holiness—without it no one will see the Lord (Hebrews 12:14 CSB).

But just as he who called you is holy, so be holy in all you do; for it is written: "Be holy, because I am holy." Since you call on a Father who judges each person's work impartially, live your lives as strangers here in reverent fear (1 Peter 1:15-17 NIV).

EMULATE THE BEATITUDES

The Beatitudes emphasize the importance of being humble, seeking righteousness, being merciful, keeping your heart pure, spreading peace, and standing up for righteousness. Many other verses do so as well, but by stringing these qualities together in this sermon Jesus paints a vivid picture of what a true Christian looks like.

Christian author, philosopher, and professor Dallas Willard said, "[The beatitudes] serve to clarify Jesus' fundamental message: the free availability of God's rule and righteousness to all of humanity through reliance upon Jesus Himself... They do this simply by taking those who, from the human point of view, are regarded as most hopeless, most beyond all possibility of God's blessing or even interest, and exhibiting them as enjoying God's touch and abundant provision from the heavens."[9]

Jesus:

"Blessed are the poor in spirit, for the kingdom of heaven is theirs. Blessed are those who mourn, for they will be comforted. Blessed are the humble, for they will inherit the earth. Blessed are those who hunger and thirst for righteousness, for they will be filled. Blessed are the merciful, for they will be shown mercy. Blessed are the pure in heart, for they will see God. Blessed are the peacemakers, for they will be called sons of God. Blessed are those who are persecuted because of righteousness, for the kingdom of heaven is theirs" (Matthew 5:3-10 CSB).

BE HUMBLE

Humility has a significant benefit: "it appears to strengthen social bonds, especially in important relationships that may experience conflict, or where differences might threaten the security of the relationship."[10] Arrogance, on the other hand, has significant detriments. "Arrogant people are less liked by others, and perceived as less sociable, less intelligent, and less productive."[11]

As unattractive as arrogance is, one would think there would be less of it. To the contrary. A recent survey revealed that "84% of the respondents reported encountering arrogant behavior at least once a month, and as many as 46% of the respondents admitted behaving arrogantly themselves."[12]

No wonder Jesus emphasized the importance of being humble in the life of a person who wants to conduct themselves as Jesus did.

Jesus:

"Whoever becomes humble like this child is the greatest in the kingdom of heaven" (Matthew 18:4 NRSV).

"Whoever exalts himself will be humbled, and whoever humbles himself will be exalted" (Matthew 23:12 CSB).

"When you are invited by someone to a wedding banquet, do not sit down at the place of honor, in case someone more distinguished than you has been invited by your host; and the host who invited both of you may come and say to you, 'Give this person your place,' and then in disgrace you would start to take the lowest place. But when you are invited, go and sit down at the lowest place, so that when your host comes, he may say to you, 'Friend, move up higher'; then you will be honored in the presence of all who sit at the table with you. For all who exalt themselves will be humbled, and those who humble themselves will be exalted" (Luke 14:8-11 NRSV).

"Everyone who exalts himself will be humbled, but the one who humbles himself will be exalted." Luke 18:14 CSB

Disciples:

Do not think of yourself more highly than you ought, but rather think of yourself with sober judgment, in accordance with the faith God has distributed to each of you (Romans 12:3 NIV).

Do not be proud; instead, associate with the humble. Do not be wise in your own estimation (Romans 12:16 CSB).

Be completely humble and gentle (Ephesians 4:2 NIV).

Do nothing out of selfish ambition or conceit, but in humility consider others as more important than yourselves (Philippians 2:3 CSB).

Humble yourself before the Lord, and he will exalt you (James 4:10 CSB).

All of you, clothe yourselves with humility toward one another, because, "God opposes the proud but shows favor to the humble." Humble yourselves, therefore, under God's mighty hand, that he may lift you up in due time (1 Peter 5:5-6 NIV).

SERVE OTHERS

It may not seem like it, but serving others is actually an act of self-improvement. "Studies indicate that the very act of giving back to the community boosts your happiness, health, and sense of well-being."[13] Apart from the obvious benefit of improving the lives of those you serve, the benefits of serving others include: living longer; causing others to serve as well; being happier; relieving pain; lowering blood pressure; promoting positive behaviors; and providing a sense of purpose and satisfaction.[14]

Jesus instructs Christians to serve others in the same manner that he did. Isn't it just like God to find a way to cause the act of helping others to improve your own life as well?

Jesus:

Jesus called them over said, "You know that the rulers of the Gentiles lord it over them, and those in high positions act as tyrants over them. It must not be like that among you. On the contrary, whoever wants to become great among you must be your servant, and whoever wants to be first among you must be your slave; just as the Son of Man did not come to be served, but to serve, and to give his life as a ransom for many" (Matthew 20:25-28 CSB).

"The greatest among you will be your servant" (Matthew 23:11 NIV).

Sitting down, he called the Twelve and said to them, "If anyone wants to be first, he must be last and servant of all" (Mark 9:35 CSB)

"But whoever wishes to become great among you must be your servant, and whoever wishes to be first among you must be slave of all. For the Son of Man came not to be served but to serve, and to give his life a ransom for many" (Mark 10:43-45 NRSV).

"Now that I, your Lord and Teacher, have washed your feet, you also should wash one another's feet. I have set you an example that you should do as I have done for you. Very truly I tell you, no servant is greater than his master, nor is a messenger greater than the one who sent him. Now that you know these things, you will be blessed if you do them" (John 13:14-17 NIV).

Disciples:

Submit to one another out of reverence for Christ (Ephesians 5:21 NIV).

Everyone should look out not only for his own interests, but also for the interests of others. Adopt the same attitude as that of Christ Jesus, who, existing in the form of God, did not consider equality with God as something to be exploited. Instead he emptied himself by assuming the form of a servant, taking on the likeness of humanity. And when he had come as a man, he humbled himself by becoming obedient to the point of death—even to death on a cross (Philippians 2:4-8 CSB).

Just as each one has received a gift, use it to serve others, as good stewards of the varied grace of God (1 Peter 4:10 CSB).

BE MERCIFUL

In October 2006, a man named Charles Roberts entered an

Amish schoolhouse in Pennsylvania. He shot ten schoolgirls, five of whom died, and then took his own life—leaving his wife, Marie, a widow and his children fatherless.

Hours later, still grieving the loss of their own children, members of the Amish community walked up Marie's sidewalk. Not to rail at her about her husband's horrific acts, but instead to inquire about her and her children, and to support them in their own time of crisis.[15] In fact, when photographers later attempted to take pictures of Roberts' family on the way to his funeral, members of the Amish community surrounded the family so the only pictures taken were of the Amish, not the grieving family.[16]

Of this Marie said: "And it was amazing. It was one of those moments during the week where my breath was taken away, but not because of the evil. But because of the love."[17]

Acts of great mercy are possible, but the circumstances that make them great also make them difficult to perform. Being merciful is a defining, if not easy, Christian trait.

Jesus:

"Be merciful, just as your Father is merciful" (Luke 6:36 NRSV).

Disciples:

Have mercy on those who waver, save others by snatching them from the fire (Jude 1:22-23 CSB).

BE CHARITABLE WITH YOUR EARNINGS

Americans give 2.1% of their disposable income to charity, on average.[18] In 2014, that translated into just over one thousand dollars for the average adult and two thousand for the average household.[19] Between 2000 and 2014, the percentage of U.S. households that donated anything to charity fell from two thirds to just over half.[20]

About a third of charitable donations are to religious organizations.[21] While eighty percent of all Americans give two percent of their incomes to charity, Christians on average give only half a percent more—two and a half percent.[22] Even among families with high incomes, over seventy five thousand dollars, only one percent of them tithe 10% or more.[23] By one account, of the 247 million Americans who identify as Christian, only 1.5 million (about half a percent) tithe.[24] If all Christians tithed a minimum of ten percent of their incomes, an additional $165 billion would be available to churches for their missions.[25]

But the trend is away from this lofty goal, not toward it. As the number of Americans who identify as "religious" falls, the amount of money people contribute to religious causes has fallen even more: such giving is down fifty percent since 1990.[26] We need to reverse this trend. Reversing it starts with me. And with you.

Disciples:

You will be enriched in every way so that you can be generous on every occasion, and through us your generosity will result in thanksgiving to God (2 Corinthians 9:11 NIV).

Let the thief no longer steal. Instead, he is to do honest work with his own hands, so that he has something to share with anyone in need (Ephesians 4:28 CSB).

Instruct those who are rich in the present age not to be arrogant or to set their hope on the uncertainty of wealth, but on God, who richly provides us with all things to enjoy. Instruct them to do what is good, to be rich in good works, to be generous and willing to share, storing up treasure for themselves as a good foundation for the coming age, so that they may take hold of what is truly life (1 Timothy 6:17-19 CSB).

BE QUIETLY COMPASSIONATE AND GENEROUS

It's great to be compassionate and generous. Many of us often perform acts of kindness and generosity. But we can reduce the value of those acts to us as Christians, and more importantly to God, by telling others about them. People sometimes do that to cause others to think more highly of them.

By all means, do nice things for people. Be generous with both your time and your money. These verses make it clear that's part of your job as a Christian. But they also say that you should do this privately, not to show off or have something to brag about.

Jesus:

"Give to the one who asks you, and do not turn away from the one who wants to borrow from you" (Matthew 5:42 NIV).

"Be careful not to practice your righteousness in front of others to be seen by them. Otherwise, you have no reward with your Father in heaven. So whenever you give to the poor, don't sound a trumpet before you, as the hypocrites do in the synagogues and on the streets, to be applauded by people. Truly I tell you, they have their reward. But when you give to the poor, don't let your left hand know what your right hand is doing, so that your giving may be in secret. And your Father who sees in secret will reward you" (Matthew 6:1-4 CSB).

"Whoever welcomes you welcomes me, and whoever welcomes me welcomes the one who sent me. Whoever welcomes a prophet in the name of a prophet will receive a prophet's reward; and whoever welcomes a righteous person in the name of a righteous person will receive the reward of the righteous; and whoever gives even a cup of cold water to one of these little ones in the name of a disciple—truly I tell you, none of these will lose their reward" (Matthew 10:40-42 NRSV).

"When the Son of Man comes in his glory, and all the angels with him, then he will sit on his glorious throne. All nations will be gathered before him, and he will separate them one from another, just as a shepherd separates the sheep from the goats. He will put the sheep on his right and the goats on the left. Then the King will say to those on his right, 'Come, you who are blessed by my Father: inherit the kingdom prepared for you from the

foundation of the world. For I was hungry and you gave me something to eat; I was thirsty and you gave me something to drink; I was a stranger and you took me in; I was naked and you clothed me; I was sick and you took care of me; I was in prison and you visited me.' Then the righteous will answer him, 'Lord, when did we see you hungry and feed you, or thirsty and give you something to drink? When did we see you a stranger and take you in, or without clothes and clothe you? When did we see you sick, or in prison, and visit you?' And the King will answer them, 'Truly I tell you, whatever you did for one of the least of these brothers and sisters of mine, you did for me.' Then he will also say to those on the left, 'Depart from me, you who are cursed, into the eternal fire prepared for the devil and his angels! For I was hungry and you gave me nothing to eat; I was thirsty and you gave me nothing to drink; I was a stranger and you didn't take me in; I was naked and you didn't clothe me, sick and in prison and you didn't take care of me.' Then they too will answer, 'Lord when did we see you hungry, or thirsty, or a stranger, or without clothes, or sick, or in prison, and not help you?' Then he will answer them, 'Truly I tell you, whatever you did not do for one of the least of these, you did not do for me.' And they will go away into eternal punishment, but the righteous into eternal life" (Matthew 25:31-46 CSB).

"Truly I tell you, anyone who gives you a cup of water in my name because you belong the Messiah will certainly not lose their reward" (Mark 9:41 NIV).

He replied to them, "The one who has two shirts must share with someone who has none, the one who has food must do the same" (Luke 3:11 CSB).

"Sell your possessions and give to the poor. Provide purses for yourselves that will not wear out, a treasure in heaven that will never fail, where no thief comes near and no moth destroys. For where your treasure is, there your heart will be also" (Luke 12:33-34 NIV).

He also said to the one who had invited him, "When you give a lunch or a dinner, don't invite your friends, your brothers or your sisters; your relatives, or your rich neighbors, because they might invite you back, and you would be repaid. On the contrary, when you host a banquet, invite those who are poor, maimed, lame, or blind and you will be blessed, because they cannot repay you; for you will be repaid at the resurrection of the righteous" (Luke 14:12-14 CSB).

Disciples:

All the believers were together and had everything in common. They sold property and possessions to give to anyone who had need (Acts 2: 44-45 NIV).

Now the entire group of those who believed were of one heart and mind, and no one claimed that any of his possessions was his own, but instead they held everything in common (Acts 4:32 CSB).

There was not a needy person among them, for as many as owned lands or houses sold them and brought the proceeds of what was sold. They laid it at the apostles' feet, and it was distributed to each as any had need (Acts 4:34-35 NRSV).

Share with the saints in their needs; pursue hospitality (Romans 12:13 CSB).

Nobody should seek their own good, but the good of others (1 Corinthians 10:24 NIV).

Remember this: Whoever sows sparingly will also reap sparingly, and whoever sows generously will also reap generously. Each of you should give what you have decided in your heart to give, not reluctantly or under compulsion, for God loves a cheerful giver (2 Corinthians 9:6-7 NIV).

You will be enriched in every way for all generosity, which produces thanksgiving to God through us (2 Corinthians 9:11 CSB).

Through the testing of this ministry you glorify God by your obedience to the confession of the gospel of Christ and by the generosity of your sharing with them and with all others, while they long for you and pray for you because of the surpassing grace of God that he has given you (2 Corinthians 9:13-14 NRSV).

Carry one another's burdens; in this way you will fulfill the law of Christ (Galatians 6:2 CSB).

Therefore, as we have opportunity, let us do good to all people, especially to those who belong to the family of believers (Galatians 6:10 NIV).

Let the thief no longer steal. Instead, he is to do honest work with his own hands, so that he has something to share with anyone in need (Ephesians 4:28 CSB).

Offer hospitality to one another without grumbling (1 Peter 4:9 NIV).

Do not neglect to do good and to share what you have, for such sacrifices are pleasing to God (Hebrews 13:16 NRSV).

If anyone has this world's goods and sees a fellow believer in need but withholds compassion for him — how does God's love reside in him? (1 John 3:17 CSB)

FORGIVE

It is hard to find a better modern-day example of forgiveness than the story of Mary Johnson, whose 20-year-old son was fatally shot by 16-year-old Oshea Israel in 1993. Mary hated Oshea for what he had done. "I wanted him to be caged up like the animal he was."[27] After many years, she decided to try to find a way to forgive him; she asked Oshea to meet with her while he was still in prison. He eventually agreed. Mary visited Oshea regularly and, when he was released, arranged for him to live in the apartment next to hers. They became close friends.[28]

Although Mary attributes this incredible act of forgiveness to her strong faith, she admits that she derived a personal benefit from it as well. "Unforgiveness is like cancer. It will eat you from the inside out. It's not about that other person, me forgiving him does not diminish what he's done. Yes, he murdered my son—but the forgiveness is for me."[29]

God wants you to forgive others. Do it for him. Do it for them. Do it for you.

Jesus:

"For if you forgive other people when they sin against you, your heavenly Father will also forgive you. But if you do not forgive others their sins, your Father will not forgive your sins" (Matthew 6:14-15 NIV).

Then Peter approached him and asked, "Lord, how many times shall I forgive my brother or sister who sins against me? As many as seven times? "I tell you, not as many as seven," Jesus replied, "but seventy times seven" (Matthew 18:21-22 CSB).

[At the conclusion of the Parable of the Unmerciful Servant] *"Then the master called the servant in. 'You wicked servant,' he said, 'I canceled all that debt of yours because you begged me to. Shouldn't you have had mercy on your fellow servant just as I had on you?' In anger his master handed him over to the jailers to be tortured, until he should pay back all he owed. This is how my heavenly Father will treat each of you unless you forgive your brother or sister from your heart"* (Matthew 18:32-35 NIV).

"And when you stand praying, if you hold anything against anyone, forgive them, so that your Father in heaven may forgive you your sins" (Mark 11:25 NIV).

"Be on your guard. If your brother sins, rebuke him, and if he repents, forgive him. And if he sins against you seven times in a day, and comes back to you seven times, saying 'I repent,' you must forgive him" (Luke 17 3:4 CSB).

Disciples:

And be kind and compassionate to one another, forgiving one another, just as God also forgave you in Christ (Ephesians 4:32 CSB).

BE INTROSPECTIVE

God expects Christians to be introspective and self-aware. We've all met people who aren't: They act like the world is theirs and we are just living in it. They think only of themselves and have no regard for others—don't they see that?

As it turns out, probably not. "95% of people think they're self-aware, but only 10-15% truly are."[30] Why? We operate on autopilot, unaware of why and how we are behaving; we are happier when we see ourselves in a more positive light, and social media has made us even more self-absorbed.[31]

How can we be more introspective? Start with prayerfully reading scripture and asking God how what you read applies to you and your life. Listen for his answer. Meditate on the things about yourself that you are grateful for, along with the things that need work. Go for walks and consider your place in the world. God put you in this place and this time—every moment of every day—for a reason. What is it? Only you can answer that question; if you don't, it will go unanswered.

Disciples:

Examine yourselves to see whether you are in the faith; test yourselves. Do you not realize that Christ Jesus is in you—unless, of course, you fail the test? (2 Corinthians 13:5 NIV)

Let each person examine his own work, and then he can take pride in himself alone, and not compare himself with someone else. For each person will have to carry his own load (Galatians 6:4 CSB).

USE YOUR GIFTS

God gave each of us gifts. One of our obligations is to identify them and cultivate them for God's use and glory.

At age 16, Albert Einstein was a high school dropout who ran away to avoid military service. When he applied for admission to a technical school, he did well in the math and physics parts of the exam, but failed French, chemistry, and biology. After completing his education, he could not find work, and was fired even from positions tutoring children. He wound up working in a patent office before turning to his groundbreaking and history-changing work in physics.[32]

Billy Graham was born into a Christian family but was himself "an unenthusiastic Christian. He was more interested in reading history, playing baseball and dreaming of becoming a professional ballplayer. His worldliness, his father thought, was mischievous and devilish."[33] After graduating high school he sold Fuller brushes door-to-door before starting college at one institution and quickly transferring to another before deciding to become a preacher.[34]

What if these men did not use their gifts? What will a person, a community, or the world be missing—and what part of God's plan will go unaccomplished — if you do not use yours?

Disciples:

We have different gifts, according to the grace given to each of us. If your gift is prophesying, then prophesy in accordance with your faith; if it is serving, then serve; if it is teaching, then teach; if it is to encourage, then give encouragement; if it is giving, then give generously; if it is to lead, do it diligently; if it is to show mercy, do it cheerfully (Romans 12:6-8 NIV).

Just as each one has received a gift, use it to serve others, as good stewards of the varied grace of God (1 Peter 4:10 CSB).

CONTROL YOURSELF

Self-control has been described as "delay[ing] short-term gratification in favor of long-term outcomes: it is the investment of cognitive, emotional and behavioral resources to achieve a desired outcome. Self-control often involves resisting temptations and impulses, and habits that often undermine self-control.... Self-control is what helps us control our emotions and impulses which enables us to behave in socially adequate ways...' Overcoming the self's natural, impulsive nature requires self-control... Without this capacity, we would be slaves of our emotional impulses, temptations, and desires and thus unable to behave socially adequately.'"[35] Of course one would expect Christians to exercise good self-control. But doing so is good for you in ways that will improve your life, too.

People with good self-control tend to have better grades, have fewer impulse control problems, are better psychologically adjusted, report more guilt but less shame than others, have better interpersonal relationships, and are happier overall.[36] They are less likely to end up overweight, and self-control is a better predictor of academic performance than intelligence.[37]

Not surprisingly, good self-control is highly correlated with success. "Of the thousands of principles of success developed over the years, this one skill will ensure that you will accomplish great things in your life. This skill will make you reach your optimum capacity, and you'll become surprised of what you'll be capable of doing. This skill is called self-discipline."[38]

It is also not surprising that exercising good self-control is in keeping with being a Christian. We are, after all, in a continuous state of deferring the instant gratification of worldly things in favor of the long-term goals of doing God's work on earth and then spending eternity in heaven.

Disciples:

So then, let us not be like others, who are asleep, but let us be alert and self-controlled. For those who sleep, sleep at night, and those who get drunk, get drunk at night. But since we belong to the day, let us be self-controlled, putting on faith and love as a breastplate, the hope of salvation as a helmet (1 Thessalonians 5:6-8 NIV).

CHOOSE YOUR WORDS CAREFULLY

It would be hard for me to tell you which I regret more: some of the things I have *done* without thinking, or some of the things I have *said* without thinking. "Sticks and stones can break my bones, but words can never hurt me." When was that ever true? Words are powerful things, and the wrong word at the wrong time can have powerful, lasting, destructive effects.

Your words can also make others look bad. As a child, the things you say reflect well or poorly on your parents. As a husband or wife, they reflect well or poorly on your spouse. As a Christian, the things you say reflect well or poorly on your God and your soul, which he is saving from eternal damnation. The least you can do in return is not make him look bad.

Jesus:

"But I tell you that men will have to give account on the day of judgment for every careless word they have spoken. For by your words you will be acquitted, and by your words you will be condemned" (Matthew 12:36-37 NIV).

"A good person produces good of the good stored up in his heart. An evil person produces evil out of the evil stored up in his heart, for his mouth speaks from the overflow of the heart" (Luke 6:45 CSB).

"There is nothing concealed that will not be disclosed, or hidden that will not be made known. What you have said in the dark will be heard in the daylight, and what you have whispered in the ear in the inner rooms will be proclaimed from the roofs" (Luke 12:2-3 NIV).

Disciples:

No foul language should come from your mouth, but only what is good for building up someone in need, so that it gives grace to those who hear (Ephesians 4:29 CSB).

Nor should there be obscenity, foolish talk or coarse joking, which are out of place, but rather thanksgiving (Ephesians 5:4 NIV).

But now, put away all the following: anger, wrath, malice, slander, and filthy language from your mouth (Colossians 3:8 CSB).

Let your conversation be always full of grace, seasoned with salt, so that you may know how to answer everyone (Colossians 4:6 NIV).

Avoid irreverent and empty speech, since those who engage in it will produce even more godlessness, and their teaching will spread like gangrene (2 Timothy 2:16-17 CSB).

Reminded the people to...slander no one (Titus 3:1-2 NIV).

If anyone thinks he is religious without controlling his tongue, his religion is useless and he deceives himself (James 1:26 CSB).

Speak and act as those who are going to be judged by the law that gives freedom, because judgment without mercy will be shown to anyone who has not been merciful (James 2:12-13 NIV).

If anyone speaks, let it be as one who speaks God's words (1 Peter 4:11 CSB).

KEEP YOUR WORD

In the hit TV (now Netflix) show "Breaking Bad," methamphetamine cook Jesse Pinkman promises to pay someone to repair the RV he and Walter White use as a rolling meth lab, saying—with feeling, "My word is my bond." Later, in dire straits and penniless, he drives the RV off without paying, crashing through a chain link gate to make his getaway. After coming into a significant amount of ill-gotten gains, he returns to pay his debt, plus a little something extra. That was to cover the damage he caused, both to the fence and to his reputation, when he broke his word.

Not an example of a good Christian, that Jesse. But he did (eventually) keep his word, something many law-abiding citizens, including Christians, do not do. The ultimate promise is the one couples make to one another when they marry. In the US, about 40% of those couples end up divorcing.[39] Despite the implicit promises fathers make to their children, one in four American children live without a father in the home.[40] And who needs to be reminded of how quickly most people break their New Year's resolutions, which are promises to ourselves.

We depend on God to keep his promises and have confidence that he will. It makes perfect sense that he would want everyone to know that they can depend on his emissaries, Christians, to do the same.

Jesus:

"Again, you have heard that it was said to the people long ago, 'Do not break your oath, but fulfill to the Lord the vows you have made.' But I tell you, do not swear an oath at all; either by heaven, for it is God's throne; or by the earth, for it is his foot stool; or by Jerusalem, for it is the city of the Great King. And do not swear by your head, for you cannot make even one hair white or black. All you need to say is simply 'Yes' or 'No'; anything beyond this comes from the evil one" (Matthew 5:33-37 NIV).

TREAT YOUR FAMILY WELL

In a world of heartbreaking stories, among the most heart-breaking are those that involve abused or neglected family members, particularly children. You may not be able to count on being safe anywhere else, but you should at least be confident you will be safe when you are at home.

And that's a minimum. You should also be able to count on your family to lift you up, educate you, teach you to be moral, and be there for you when you are in need. Your family should be able to count on you to do these things for them, too.

Jesus:

"Honor your father and your mother" (Matthew 19:19 CSB).

Disciples:

Wives, submit to your husbands as to the Lord. For the husband is the head of the wife as Christ is the head of the church, his body, of which he is the Savior. Now as the church submits to Christ, so also wives should submit to their husbands in everything (Ephesians 5:22-24 NIV).

Husbands, love your wives, just as Christ loved the church and gave himself for her to make her holy, cleansing her with the washing of water by the word. He did this to present the church to himself in splendor, without spot or wrinkle or anything like that, but holy and blameless. In the same way, husbands are to love their wives as their own bodies. He who loves his wife loves himself (Ephesians 5:25-28 CSB).

To sum up, each one of you is to love his wife as himself, and the wife is to respect her husband (Ephesians 5:33 CSB).

Children, obey your parents in the Lord, for this is right. "Honor your father and mother"—which is the first commandment with a promise—"that it may go well with you and that you may enjoy long life on the earth." Fathers, do not exasperate your children; instead bring them up in the training and instruction of the Lord (Ephesians 6:1-4 NIV).

[An overseer] must manage his own household competently and have his children under control with all dignity. (If anyone does not know how to manage his own household, how will he take care of God's church?) (1 Timothy 3:4-5 CSB)

But if a widow has children or grandchildren, these should learn first of all to put their religion into practice by caring for their own family and so repaying their parents and grandparents, for this is pleasing to God (1 Timothy 5:4 NIV).

But if anyone does not provide for his own family, especially for his own household, he has denied the faith and is worse than an unbeliever (1 Timothy 5:8 CSB).

Teach the older men to be temperate, worthy of respect, self-controlled, and sound in faith, in love and in endurance. Likewise, teach the older women to be reverent in the way they live, not to be slanderers or addicted to much wine, but to teach what is good. Then they can urge the younger women to love their husbands and children, to be self-controlled and pure, to be busy at home, to be kind, and to be subject to their husbands (Titus 2:2-5 NIV).

TURN THE OTHER CHEEK

Now this is a hard one. How can you possibly get along in today's society if you let other people walk all over you? The following verses help us understand that the first step is not to think about it that way.

As is true of all things that are part of God's plan, when someone wrongs you, you are in just another situation that God intends for good. He intends your reaction to glorify him, to bless you, and to give him the opportunity to work a change in the wrongdoer. Aren't those things more important than retaliating when someone has wronged you?

The next step is to realize that the behavior God expects of you is not subject to exceptions. You are not to be kind to people only if they are kind to you. You are not to be loving only to those who are loving toward you. It's easy to be on Christ-like behavior when those around you are; anyone can do that. Your ability to act as Jesus taught is tested when those around you are not behaving that way. If you reduce the quality of your behavior to the depths of the bad behavior others are capable of, how is that remotely in keeping with your status as a Christian?

Finally, part of your job as a Christian is to reduce the temperature in a hot room, not raise it. As verses we covered earlier make clear, God wants you to be a peacemaker. If you respond in kind to personal attacks, you will not only contribute to, but worsen, a state of affairs that God doesn't want to exist in the first place.

A great example of a Christian repeatedly turning the other cheek and, by doing so, finding success and glorifying God, is that of Jackie Robinson. When he was given the opportunity to break major league baseball's color barrier, it was clear that the experiment would fail miserably if he responded in kind to anticipated mistreatment by prejudiced baseball fans.[41] He didn't, and instead prayed every night for the strength it took to bear the burden he willingly, and successfully, undertook.[42]

Chances are, you will never be punched in the mouth and have to decide whether to hit back. Instead, you probably face less dramatic moments and decisions, but face them often. Someone cutting you off in traffic, or eating your lunch out of the refrigerator at work. Insulting you or your group online. Gossiping about you.

Be sure anyone watching can tell which of the participants in those uncomfortable situations is acting as Jesus would.

Jesus:

"You have heard that it was said, An eye for an eye and a tooth for a tooth. But I tell you, don't resist an evildoer. On the contrary, if anyone slaps you on your right cheek, turn the other to him also. As for the one who wants to sue you and take away your shirt, let him have your coat as well. And if anyone forces you to go one mile, go with him two. Give to the one who asks you, and don't turn away from the one who wants to borrow from you. You have heard that it was said, Love your neighbor and hate your enemy. But I tell you, love your enemies and pray for those who persecute you, so that you may be children of your Father in heaven" (Matthew 5:38-45 CSB).

Disciples:

Bless those who persecute you; bless and do not curse (Romans 12:14 NIV).

Do not repay anyone evil for evil (Romans 12:17 CSB).

And the Lord's servant must not be quarrelsome but kindly to everyone, an apt teacher, patient, correcting opponents with gentleness. God may perhaps grant that they will repent and come to know the truth, and that they may escape from the snare of the devil, having been held captive by him to do his will (2 Timothy 2:24-26 NRSV).

...not paying back evil for evil or insult for insult but, on the contrary, giving a blessing, since you were called for this, so that you may inherit a blessing (1 Peter 3:9 CSB).

PRAY

While turning the other cheek may be a tough thing to do, you'll be pleased to learn that the next thing Christians are supposed to do is the easiest, and something you probably do with some regularity: pray. Over half of adults pray at least daily, only about a quarter seldom or never.[43] Ninety percent of adult Jehovah's Witnesses, eighty five percent of adult Mormons, and seventy nine percent of adult evangelical Protestants pray at least daily; fifty nine percent of Catholics and fifty seven percent of Orthodox Christians do.[44] "Prayer is by far the most common spiritual practice among Americans... The vast majority of Americans—no matter their religious affiliation or non-affiliation—participate in some kind of prayer activity." [45]

Jesus and his disciples encouraged Christians to pray under all circumstances and assured Christians that prayer is powerful and meaningful. Like being generous and compassionate, however, Jesus taught us to pray privately, not in a manner that is a form of bragging or that is designed to show others how devout we are.

And, in fact, that is the way most people pray. Ninety four percent of adult Americans who pray choose to pray by themselves.[46] Eighty two percent most often pray silently, as opposed to audibly; only two percent pray audibly with another person or group, or collectively with a church.[47]

Your prayers probably include a lot of "pleases" and "thank yous." "Gratitude and thanksgiving" is the most common type of prayer, with "the needs of my family and community," "personal guidance in crisis," and "my health and wellness" following close behind.[48] Forty three percent of praying adults' prayers most often relate to "confession and forgiveness," and thirty seven percent "a sense of peace."[49] As to the pleases and thank yous: You can probably find a reason to send up far more of the latter than the former if you look hard enough.

Jesus:

"And when you pray, do not be like the hypocrites, for they love to pray standing in the synagogues and on the street corners to be seen by others. Truly I tell you, they have received their reward in full. But when you pray, go into your room, close the door and pray to your Father, who is unseen. Then your Father, who sees what is done in secret, will reward you. And when you pray, do not keep on babbling like pagans, for they think they will be heard because of their many words. Do not be like them, for your Father knows what you need before you ask him" (Matthew 6:5-8 NIV).

"And if you believe, you will receive whatever you ask for in prayer" (Matthew 21:22 CSB).

"So I tell you, whatever you ask for in prayer, believe that you have received it, and it will be yours" (Mark 11:24 NRSV).

Disciples:

Rejoice in the hope; be patient in affliction; be persistent in prayer (Romans 12:12 CSB).

Do not be anxious about anything, but in everything, by prayer and petition, with thanksgiving, present your requests to God (Philippians 4:6 NIV).

Devote yourselves to prayer; stay alert in it with thanksgiving (Colossians 4:2 CSB).

Rejoice always, pray constantly, give thanks in everything; for this is God's will for you in Christ Jesus (1 Thessalonians 5:16-18 CSB).

Are any among you suffering? They should pray. Are any cheerful? They should sing songs of praise. Are any among you sick? They should call for the elders of the church and have them pray over them, anointing them with oil in the name of the Lord. The prayer of faith will save the sick, and the Lord will raise them up; and anyone who has committed sins will be forgiven (James 5:13-15 NRSV).

The end of all things is near; therefore, be alert and sober-minded for prayer (1 Peter 4:7 CSB).

But you, beloved, build yourselves up on your most holy faith; pray in the Holy Spirit (Jude 1:20 NRSV).

ACKNOWLEDGE CHRIST

Consider who Jesus is, what he taught, and what he did. Consider that, by becoming a Christian, a person aligns themselves with Christ and commits themselves to living as he taught and as he lived.

Now consider that, to many people, "Christian" is a dirty word. How can that be?

But things are actually much worse than that. Around the world, acknowledging Christ has become a dangerous endeavor. It has cost many Christians their lives. A 2019 headline on BBC News reads: "Christian persecution 'at near genocide levels.'"[50] The article explains that, by virtue of Christians fleeing persecution, Christianity is at risk of disappearing in some parts of the world.[51] "Evidence shows not only the geographic spread of anti-Christian persecution, but also its increasing severity... In some regions, the level and nature of persecution is arguably coming close to meeting the international definition of genocide, according to that adopted by the UN."[52]

In America, the situation is better for Christians, using hate crimes as a proxy for persecution, but better does not mean "good." In 2018, there were 835 anti-Jewish and 188 anti-Islamic hate crimes reported, compared to 53 anti-Catholic, 35 anti-"other Christian," and 34 anti-Protestant.[53] Attacks on Christians persisted in 2020. Protestors burned Bibles in Portland, Oregon.[54] Someone burned down a Pentecostal church in Mississippi, apparently because its leaders filed a lawsuit challenging restrictions that prevented them from holding services during the COVID-19 pandemic.[55] A number of other churches and Christian symbols were attacked, burned, and vandalized during the summer of 2020 for other reasons.[56]

American Christians are increasingly the subject of other forms of ridicule and mistreatment as well. A "new vigorous secularism has catapulted mockery of Christianity and other forms of religious traditionalism into the mainstream and set a new low for what counts as civil criticism of people's most-cherished beliefs.... Anti-Christian activists hurl smears like 'bigot' and 'hater' at Americans who hold traditional beliefs about marriage and accuse anti-abortion Christians of waging a supposed 'war on women.'"[57] Your own experience probably confirms that it is becoming increasingly difficult and hazardous for Christians to publicly acknowledge their faith and beliefs.

But publicly acknowledge them, and Jesus, we must. We owe it to ourselves, to our brothers and sisters in faith, and to non-believers who depend on us to lead them to Christ to fight back against those who would intimidate us into silence and submission. Take courage and inspiration from other proud Christians; then return the favor.

Jesus:

"Therefore, everyone who will acknowledge me before others, I will also acknowledge him before my Father in heaven. But who-

ever denies me before others, I will also deny him before my Father in heaven" (Matthew 10:32-33 CSB).

"Whoever is ashamed of me and my words, the Son of Man will be ashamed of them when he comes in his glory and in the glory of the Father and of the holy angels" (Luke 9:26 NIV).

"And I say to you, anyone who acknowledges me before others, the Son of Man will also acknowledge him before the angels of God, but whoever denies me before others will be denied before the angels of God" (Luke 12:8-9 CSB).

God did not give us a spirit of cowardice, but rather a spirit of power and of love and of self-discipline. Do not be ashamed, then, of the testimony about our Lord (2 Timothy 1:7-8 NRSV).

OBEY THOSE IN AUTHORITY

You may find yourself swallowing hard when you read these verses. Politicians, people, and our perspectives on many issues have become so polarized that you may find yourself not wanting to even listen to, much less obey, some of those who are in authority.

But breaking the law is not an option for Christians. Try to vote people you disagree with out of office if you want, but while they hold office the following verses compel you to obey them.

Disciples:

Let everyone be subject to the governing authorities, for there is no authority except that which God has established. The authorities that exist have been established by God. Consequently, whoever rebels against the authority is rebelling against what God has instituted, and those who do so will bring judgment on themselves.... Therefore, it is necessary to submit to the authorities, not only because of possible punishment but also as a matter of conscience (Romans 13:1-2, 5 NIV).

Submit to every human authority because of the Lord, whether to the Emperor as the supreme authority or to governors as those sent out by him to punish those who do what is evil and to praise those who do what is good (1 Peter 2:13-14 CSB).

GRATEFULLY REJOICE

We touched on gratitude in connection with praying. This "do" involves rejoicing and worshiping God for the extraordinary gift he has given you: a richly rewarding life on earth and eternal life thereafter. To rejoice means to experience great joy or delight, and also to express it. As Christians, we certainly have good reason to do both.

To experience the great joy and delight associated with being a Christian is pretty easy; if you think about it enough, these emotions naturally follow. Try adding all of the wonderful things that come with being a Christian to the matters you spend time thinking about each day.

But it is hard to find ways to express your joy when going about your daily life, with all of its responsibilities, tensions, and distractions. And there's the reaction you may draw from some people if you just walk up and tell them how happy you are about being a Christian. (Not that that makes it a bad idea...) It is easy at church, however, where everyone sings hymns or praise and worship songs whose content often includes rejoicing.

You probably listen to music at some point in your day (if you don't, I recommend that you start). Find a station that plays praise and worship. Add favorite hymns or contemporary Christian songs to your playlist. Sing along enthusiastically. By doing so, you will engage in the deep and rewarding practice of rejoicing; joyfully expressing your profound gratitude to God for all that he has done for you. C.S. Lewis said:

> I think we delight to praise what we enjoy because the praise not merely expresses but completes the enjoyment; it is its appointed consummation. It is not out of compliment that lovers keep on telling one another how beautiful they are; the delight is incomplete until it is expressed. It is frustrating to have discovered a

new author and not be able to tell anyone how good he is; to come suddenly, at the turn of the road, upon some mountain valley of unexpected grandeur and then have to keep silent because the people with you care for it no more than for a tin can in the ditch; to hear a good joke and find no one to share it with...The Scotch catechism says that man's chief end is 'to glorify God and enjoy him forever.' But we shall then know that these are the same thing. Fully to enjoy is to glorify. In commanding us to glorify Him, God is inviting us to enjoy Him.[58]

Rejoicing: it's not just for church anymore.

Disciples:

We boast in our hope of sharing the glory of God. And not only that, but we also boast in our sufferings, knowing that suffering produces endurance, and endurance produces character, and character produces hope, and hope does not disappoint us, because God's love has been poured into our hearts through the Holy Spirit that has been given to us (Romans 5:2-5 NRSV).

Finally, my brothers and sisters, rejoice in the Lord (Philippians 3:1 NRSV).

Rejoice in the Lord always. I will say it again: Rejoice! (Philippians 4:4 CSB).

So then, just as you have received Christ Jesus as Lord, continue to live in him, being rooted and built up in him and established in the faith, just as you were taught, and overflowing with gratitude (Colossians 2:6-7 CSB).

Let the peace of Christ rule in your hearts, since as members of one body you were called to peace. And be thankful (Colossians 3:15 NIV).

And whatever you do, in word or in deed, do everything in the name of the Lord Jesus, giving thanks to God the Father through him (Colossians 3:17 CSB).

Sing and make music from your heart to the Lord, always giving thanks to God the Father for everything, in the name of our Lord Jesus Christ (Ephesians 5:19-20 NIV).

Rejoice always, pray constantly, give thanks in everything; for this is God's will for you in Christ Jesus (1 Thessalonians 5:16-18 CSB).

Those are the dos; there are a lot of them. You will be pleased to learn that there are fewer don'ts. Perhaps that's because, if you are doing the dos, you won't be doing the don'ts.

18

Christian Don'ts

DON'T JUDGE

We know we are not supposed to, but, of course, we tend to judge one another. People always have and probably always will. But people have used the advent of social media to turn judging others into an art form.

Social media outlets are judgment factories, where events are publicized, judgments passed, sentences read, and sentences carried out — virtually instantaneously. By people who may not know the first thing about what really happened, without reflection, without compassion, without mercy or forgiveness, without introspection or self-control, and in language they often soon regret. A common sentence that follows social media judgment these days is being "cancelled," by being fired, boycotted, ostracized, unfriended, blocked, or whatever other form it may take in a given person's life.

It's an absolutely awful, toxic practice that has taken hold and is thriving in our society. Combat it if you can, but your first obligation as a Christian is not to contribute to it. If you help produce the products manufactured in a judgment factory, put these verses by your device and reflect on them before you post.

Jesus:

"Do not judge, or you too will be judged. For in the same way you judge others, you will be judged, and with the measure you use, it will be measured to you. Why do you look at the speck of sawdust in your brother's eye and pay no attention to the plank in your own eye? How can you say to your brother, 'let me take the speck out of your eye,' when all the time there is a plank in your own eye? You hypocrite, first take the plank out of your own

eye, and then you will see clearly to remove the speck from your brother's eye" (Matthew 7:1-5 NIV).

"Do not judge, and you will not be judged. Do not condemn, and you will not be condemned. Forgive, and you will be forgiven. Give, and it will be given to you; a good measure—pressed down, shaken together, and running over—will be poured into your lap. For with the measure you use, it will be measured back to you" (Luke 6:37-38 CSB).

Disciples:

You, therefore, have no excuse, you who pass judgment on someone else, for at whatever point you judge another, you are condemning yourself, because you who pass judgment do the same things. Now we know that God's judgment against those who do such things is based on truth. So when you, a mere human being, pass judgment on them and yet do the same things, do you think you will escape God's judgment? (Romans 2:1-3 NIV)

Let us therefore no longer pass judgment on one another, but resolve instead never to put a stumbling block or hindrance in the way of another (Romans 14:13 NRSV).

DON'T WORRY IN GENERAL

"Don't worry; be happy." Thanks, Bobby McFerrin, for a great message. If only it were that simple.

Anxiety disorders are the most common mental illness in the U.S., affecting 40 million adults in the United States age 18 and older, or 18.1% of the population every year.[59]

This is especially unfortunate in light of the physical toll worrying can take on the worrier.

Chronic worrying can affect your daily life so much that it may interfere with your appetite, lifestyle habits, relationships, sleep, and job performance. Many people who worry excessively are so anxiety-ridden that they seek relief in harmful lifestyle habits such as overeating, cigarette smoking, or using alcohol and drugs.[60]

The stress hormones that worry dumps into your brain have been linked to shrinking brain mass, lowering your IQ, being prone to heart disease, cancer and premature aging, predicting marital problems, family dysfunction and clinical depression, and making seniors more likely to develop dementia and Alzheimer's.[61]

As it turns out, most of this worry is a complete waste of time. A recent study demonstrated that eighty five percent of what people worried about didn't happen.[62]

It's bad for you, it's a waste of time, and God doesn't want you to do it. So, don't worry, be happy.

Jesus:

"Therefore I tell you, do not worry about your life, what you will eat or drink; or about your body, what you will wear. Is not life more than food, and the body more than clothes? Look at the birds of the air; they do not sow or reap or store away in barns, and yet your heavenly Father feeds them. Are you not much more valuable than they? Can any one of you by worrying add a single hour to your life?" (Matthew 6:25-27 NIV).

"Therefore don't worry about tomorrow, because tomorrow will worry about itself. Each day has enough trouble of its own" (Matthew 6:34 CSB).

"And can any of you by worrying add a single hour to your span of life? If then you are not able to do so small a thing as that, why do you worry about the rest?" (Luke 12:25-26 NRSV)

"Don't strive for what you should eat and what you should drink, and don't be anxious. For the Gentile world eagerly seeks all these things, and your Father knows that you need them. But seek his kingdom and these things will be provided for you. Don't be

afraid, little flock, because your father delights to give you the kingdom" (Luke 12:29-32 CSB).

Disciples:

Do not be anxious about anything, but in every situation, by prayer and petition, with thanksgiving, present your requests to God. Philippians 4:6 NIV

Humble yourselves, therefore, under the mighty hand of God, so that he may exalt you at the proper time, casting all your cares on him, because he cares about you. 1 Peter 5:6-7 CSB

Don't Worry About Money

Americans are increasingly anxious about money. New data from Northwestern Mutual's 2018 Planning & Progress Study found that money is the No. 1 cause of stress among Americans, according to 44 percent of survey respondents. Money is more of a problem than either personal relationships (25 percent) or work (18 percent).[63]

Financial stress impacts forty-one percent of American marital relationships, causes forty-five percent of Americans to miss out on social events, and causes more than a quarter of Americans to feel depressed on a monthly basis.[64] "Twenty-five percent of Americans say they worry about money 'all the time.'"[65]

Americans worry about money in good economic times and bad.

"Regardless of the economic climate, money and finances have remained the top stressor since our survey began in 2007," says APA CEO Norman B. Anderson, PhD.[66]

A 2014 study "found that 72 percent of Americans reported feeling stressed about money at least some of the time during the past month," with twenty two percent describing that stress as an extreme" 8, 9, or 10 on a 10 point scale.[67]

If you worry about money, you are in good company. But Jesus and his disciples tell us that, as a Christian, you should not concern yourself with money or accumulating wealth. God has you covered.

Jesus:

"Do not store up for yourselves treasures on earth, where moth and rust consume and where thieves break in and steal; but store up for yourselves treasures in heaven, where neither moth nor rust consumes and where thieves do not break in and steal. For where your treasure is, there your heart will be also" (Matthew 6:19-21 NRSV).

"No one can serve two masters, since either he will hate one and love the other, or he will be devoted to one and despise the other. You cannot serve both God and money" (Matthew 6:24 CSB).

"And why do you worry about clothes? See how the flowers of the field grow. They do not labor or spin. Yet I tell you that not even Solomon in all his splendor was dressed like one of these. If that is how God clothes the grass of the field, which is here today and tomorrow is thrown into the fire, will he not much more clothe you—you of little faith? So do not worry, saying, 'What shall we eat?' or 'What shall we drink?' or 'What shall we wear?' For the pagans run after all these things, and your heavenly Father knows that you need them. But seek first his kingdom and his righteousness, and all these things will be given to you as well" (Matthew 6:28-33 NIV).

"If you want to be perfect," Jesus said to him, *"go, sell your belongings and give to the poor, and you will have treasure in heaven. Then come, follow me." When the young man heard that, he went away grieving, because he had many possessions. Jesus said to his disciples, "Truly I tell you, it will be hard for a rich person to enter the kingdom of heaven. Again I tell you, it is easier for a camel to go through the eye of a needle than for a rich person to enter the kingdom of God"* (Matthew 19:21-24 CSB). See also Mark 10:21-25; Luke 18:22-25.

"Watch out! Be on your guard against all kinds of greed; life does not consist in an abundance of possessions" (Luke 12:15 NIV).

"But God said to him, 'You fool! This very night your life is de-manded of you. And the things you have prepared—whose will they be?' That's how it is with the one who stores up treasure for himself and is not rich toward God" (Luke 12:20-21 CSB).

"So therefore, none of you can become my disciple if you do not give up all your possessions" (Luke 14:33 NRSV).

"What is highly admired by people is revolting in God's sight" (Luke 16:15 CSB).

Disciples:

Yet whatever gains I had, these I have come to regard as loss be-cause of Christ. More than that, I regard everything as loss be-cause of the surpassing value of knowing Christ Jesus my Lord. For his sake I have suffered the loss of all things, and I regard them as rubbish, in order that I may gain Christ and be found in him (Philippians 3:7-9 NRSV).

Keep your life free from the love of money. Be satisfied with what you have, for he himself has said, I will never leave you or abandon you (Hebrews 13:5 CSB).

Of course, there is great gain in godliness combined with con-tentment; for we brought nothing into the world, so that we can take nothing out of it; but if we have food and clothing, we will be content with these. But those who want to be rich fall into temptation and are trapped by many senseless and harmful de-sires that plunge people into ruin and destruction. For the love of money is a root of all kinds of evil, and in their eagerness to be rich some have wandered away from the faith and pierced them-selves with many pains. But as for you, man of God, shun all this; pursue righteousness, godliness, faith, love, endurance, gen-tleness (1 Timothy 6:6-11 NRSV).

Do not love the world or the things in the world. If anyone loves the world, the love of the Father is not in him. For everything in the world—the lust of the flesh, the lust of the eyes, and the pride in one's possessions—is not from the Father, but is from the world (1 John 2:15-16 CSB).

DON'T LIE

It is inherently difficult to gather reliable information about lying; how do you know whether a person is lying moment to moment, much less how often everyone does? And if you asked a liar if they lie, would they tell you the truth? But, for whatever it's worth, there is a lot of information about lying out there.

According to one source, "we're lied to 10 to 200 times a day, and tell a lie ourselves an average of 1 to 2 times in the same period."[68] Another reports that a study revealed that "undergraduates lie to their mothers in 46 percent of their conversations" and in an eye-popping seventy seven percent of their conversations with total strangers.[69] Another study found that "60 percent of people lied at least once during a 10-minute conversation and told an average of two to three lies."[70]

Sixty percent of American adults responding to a survey claimed they had not lied in the preceding 24 hours, while the lies admitted by five percent of those surveyed accounted for half of the total.[71] This suggests that while most people lie occasionally, a few people lie often. That matches up nicely with my experience.

Jesus:

"Do not give false testimony" (Matthew 19:18 NIV).

"Do not bear false witness" (Mark 10:19 CSB).

"You shall not bear false witness" (Luke 18:20 NRSV).

Disciples:

Therefore, putting away lying, speak the truth, each one to his neighbor, because we are members of one another (Ephesians 4:25 CSB).

Do not lie to each other, since you have taken off your old self with its practices and have put on the new self, which is being renewed in knowledge in the image of its Creator (Colossians 3:9 NIV).

DON'T CHEAT

Most cultures consider adultery immoral. It is prohibited in Judaism, Christianity, Islam, Hindu, Buddhism, and Confucianism.[72] It remains criminal in many countries and even in twenty one states in the United States.[73] A global survey of three fourths of the world's population found that seventy eight percent of people agreed that "married people having an affair was morally unacceptable."[74]

However universally condemned, adultery is commonplace. "A 2005 global survey estimated that 22 percent of married people worldwide admitted to having committed adultery."[75] In 2016, a survey concluded that one or both spouses cheat in over one third of marriages.[76] In the United States, "national surveys of married couples found that 25 percent of men and 15 percent of women admitted to committing adultery."[77]

In April 2020, during the early months of the COVID-19 pandemic lockdown, membership in Ashley Madison, a matchmaking website for cheating spouses, was increasing by seventeen thousand people per day. This was on top of the sixty-five million members it sported at the end of 2019.[78]

For purposes of this book, "cheating" also includes fornication (unmarried people having sex with each other) and the catch-all of other "sexual immorality." The New Testament is just as clear that Christians should not do these things as it is they should not commit adultery. But getting unmarried people not to have sex until they are married? Admittedly, that's a heavy lift.

Not that there aren't plenty of examples of people who waited. Ben Shapiro is a conservative commentator and Orthodox Jew. He is proud of the fact that he has only had sex with one woman, his wife, and they waited until they were married to have sex. NFL star Tim Tebow, actors Jessica Simpson and Kirk Cameron, singers Julianne Hough and American Idol winner Carrie Underwood waited, too.[79]

At the other end of the spectrum, you find people who, according to published remarks, have slept with thousands of people. Rock star John Oates reportedly lost track of how many women he has slept with; "I'm sure it was thousands."[80] Reportedly, rock star Gene Simmons, almost 5000; NBA legend Wilt Chamberlain, 20,000; and Playboy magazine founder and editor-in-chief Hugh Hefner over a thousand ("How could I possibly know?").[81]

Everyone else falls somewhere in between. "Waiting until marriage for sex is relatively rare in the U.S....According to the Centers for Disease Control and Prevention, close to 90 percent of people who've ever been married say they have had premarital sex."[82] According to WaitingTillMarriage.Org, about three percent of Americans successfully wait until marriage to have sex; although that's a small percentage, it amounts to about ten million people.[83]

If you are one of them, that's something to be proud of.

Jesus:

"You have heard that it was said, 'You shall not commit adultery.' But I tell you that anyone who looks at a woman lustfully has already committed adultery with her in his heart" (Matthew 5:27-28 NIV).

Some Pharisees approached him to test him. They asked, "Is it lawful for a man to divorce his wife on any grounds?" "Haven't you read," he replied, that he who created them in the beginning made them male and female, and he also said, 'For this reason a man will leave his father and mother and be joined to his wife, and the two will become one flesh'? So they are no longer two, but one flesh. Therefore, what God has joined together, let no one separate."... "I tell you, whoever divorces his wife, except for sexual immorality, and marries another commits adultery" (Matthew 19:3-6, 9 CSB).

"Do not commit adultery" (Matthew 19:18 CSB).

Disciples:

You are to abstain from...sexual immorality. You will do well to avoid these things (Acts 15:29 NIV).

Flee sexual immorality! Every other sin a person commits is outside the body, but the person who is sexually immoral sins against his own body. Don't you know that your body is a temple of the Holy Spirit who is in you, whom you have from God? You are not your own, for you were bought at a price. So glorify God with your body (1 Corinthians 6:18-20 CSB).

To the married I give this command (not I, but the Lord): A wife must not separate from her husband. But if she does, she must remain unmarried or else be reconciled to her husband. And a husband must not divorce his wife (1 Corinthians 7:10-11 NIV).

Let us not commit sexual immorality (1 Corinthians 10:8 CSB).

Now the works of the flesh are obvious: sexual immorality, impurity, promiscuity... I am warning you about these things—as I warned you before—that those who practice such things will not inherit the kingdom of God (Galatians 5:19-21 CSB).

But among you there must not be even a hint of sexual immorality, or of any kind of impurity... because these are improper for God's holy people (Ephesians 5:3 NIV).

Therefore, put to death what belongs to your earthly nature: sexual immorality, impurity, lust, evil desire, and greed, which is idolatry (Colossians 3:5 CSB).

It is God's will that you should be sanctified: that you should avoid sexual immorality; that each of you should learn to control his own body in a way that is holy and honorable, not in passionate lust like the pagans, who do not know God (1 Thessalonians 4:3-5 NIV).

Marriage is to be honored by all and the marriage bed kept un-

defiled, because God will judge the sexually immoral and adul-terers (Hebrews 13:4 CSB).

At the risk of politicizing a book that is intended to be entirely non-political, coverage of this topic would not be complete without a few words, and a few verses, about same-sex marriage and homosexuality. First, I offer the following observations to put the issue in context.

As an institution, marriage exists in two realms: the legal and the spiritual. The boundaries of one end where the boundaries of the other begin.

In the legal realm, through a political process, voters elect public officials to pass and enforce laws. Some of those laws relate to marriage: who can and cannot be legally married; under what circumstances; with what attendant burdens and benefits; with what attendant rights and obligations. Voters can influence those laws by expressing their opinions, protesting, deciding who to vote for and persuading others to do the same, and the like. Those laws can be whatever the more powerful political forces cause them to be, and they can change with the times.

Marriage as an institution in the legal realm has legal, but not spiritual, significance. Legal marriage is designed to be available to anyone, of any faith or no faith, who wants to be part of the legal relationship marital laws create.

In the Christian spiritual realm, in contrast, God established spiritual laws that govern his people and, through Jesus and his disciples, told us what they are. Some of those laws relate to marriage and sex outside of marriage, whatever its form. God did not ask for our input regarding what his spiritual laws should be; our opinions on the subject are of no moment. We don't get to vote on God's spiritual laws. Yelling at those who disagree with our views, protesting, and demonstrating will not change spiritual laws.

Marriage as an institution in the spiritual realm has spiritual, but no legal, significance. Christian marriage is designed to be a spiritual institution available to Christians. It creates spiritual burdens and benefits, costs and obligations, but no legal rights or obligations.

So, the next time you find yourself in a discussion about homosexuality and same-sex marriage, consider drawing a distinction between what the Bible says about those things, which are immutable and spiritual, and what the law says about those things, which governments can craft however they choose and change at will.

Having said that, to equip you with knowledge of what the Bible says about those things, the following verses tell us what Jesus and his disciples said about marriage and homosexuality. Note that, in keeping with the idea that in God's eyes a sin is a sin is a sin, the verses in 1 Corinthians describe homosexuality as being on par with any other sexual immorality, theft, greed, drunkenness, verbal abuse, and other sinful behavior. In God's eyes, individuals who have homosexual sex outside of marriage are no better, and no worse, than those who have heterosexual sex outside of marriage, or commit any other sin. Food for thought.

Jesus:

"Haven't you read," he replied, "that he who created them in the beginning made them male and female, and he also said, 'For this reason a man will leave his father and mother and be joined to his wife, and the two will become one flesh'? So they are no longer two, but one flesh. Therefore, what God has joined together, let no one separate" (Matthew 19:4-6 CSB). See also Ephesians 5:31.

"But from the beginning of creation, 'God made them male and female.' 'For this reason a man shall leave his father and mother and be joined to his wife, and the two shall become one flesh.' So they are no longer two, but one flesh. Therefore what God has joined together, let no one separate" (Mark 10:6-9 NRSV).

Disciples:

The wrath of God is being revealed from heaven against all the godlessness and wickedness of people, who suppress the truth by their wickedness, since what may be known about God is plain to them, because God has made it plain to them.... Because of this, God gave them over to shameful lusts. Even their women exchanged natural sexual relations for unnatural ones. In the same way the men also abandoned natural relations with women and were inflamed with lust for one another. Men committed shameful acts with other men, and received in themselves the due penalty for their error (Romans 1:18-19, 26-27 NIV).

Don't you know that the unrighteous will not inherit God's kingdom? Do not be deceived: no sexually immoral people, idolaters, adulterers, or males who have sex with males, no thieves, greedy people, drunkards, verbally abusive people, or swindlers will inherit God's kingdom (1 Corinthians 6:9-10 CSB).

We know that the law is not meant for a righteous person, but for the lawless and rebellious, for the ungodly and sinful, for the unholy and irreverent, for those who kill their fathers and mothers, for murderers, for the sexually immoral and homosexuals, for slave traders, liars, perjurers, and for whatever else is contrary to the sound teaching that conforms to the gospel concerning the glory of the blessed God, which was entrusted to me (1 Timothy 1:9-11 CSB).

Likewise, Sodom and Gomorrah and the surrounding cities, which, in the same manner as they, indulged in sexual immorality and pursued unnatural lust, serve as an example by undergoing a punishment of eternal fire (Jude 1:7 NRSV).

DON'T STEAL

In March 2009, Bernic Madoff pleaded guilty to defrauding his clients through a Ponzi scheme; their losses were estimated to be in the range of $50 to $65 billion.[84] Most thieves are less ambitious, but there sure are a lot of them.

The FBI defines larceny-theft as the unlawful taking, carrying, leading, or riding away of property from the possession or constructive possession of another without using force, violence, or fraud; stealing cars or bikes, shoplifting, and pocket-picking, for example.[85]

The number of such crimes fell steadily between 2009 and 2018, but was still over five million in 2018.[86] In 2018, \$24.26 billion was lost to payment card fraud worldwide, with Americans bearing almost forty percent of those losses.[87]

And how many everyday thefts go undetected, by customers not returning overpayments in incorrect change, businesses adding un-earned charges to invoices, or people using other's credentials to watch Netflix? Can something you do fall into the category of theft?

Jesus:

"Do not steal" (Matthew 19:18 CSB).

"You shall not steal" (Mark 10:19 NRSV).

"Do not steal" (Luke 18:20 CSB).

Disciples:

Thieves must give up stealing (Ephesians 4:28 NRSV).

Don't Get Angry

"Anger is growing in terms of frequency, intensity and dura-tion."[88] A recent report of the Mental Health Organization revealed that "64% either strongly agree or agree that people in general are getting angrier" and "almost a third of people polled (32%) say they have a close friend or family member who has trouble controlling their anger." [89] More than a quarter of people surveyed in the UK say they worry about how angry they sometimes feel, forty five percent regularly lose their temper at work, and "more than 80% of drivers say they have been involved in road rage incidents; 25% have com-mitted an act of road rage themselves."[90]

In the first of the following verses, Jesus appears to put anger on par with murder. The next time you feel yourself getting angry with someone, picture Jesus watching you, regarding your anger with that person as the same as killing them. How angry will you let yourself get?

Jesus:

"You have heard that it was said to our ancestors, Do not murder, and whoever murders will be subject to judgment. But I tell you, everyone who is angry with his brother or sister will be subject to judgment.... Whoever says, 'You fool!' Will be subject to hellfire" (Matthew 5:21-22 CSB).

Disciples:

Now the works of the flesh are obvious:... outbursts of anger... I am warning you about these things—as I warned you before—that those who practice such things will not inherit the kingdom of God (Galatians 5:19-21 CSB).

In your anger do not sin (Ephesians 4:26 NIV).

Let all bitterness, anger and wrath, shouting and slander be removed from you, along with all malice (Ephesians 4:31 CSB).

But now you must also rid yourselves of all such things as these: anger, rage, malice, slander, and filthy language from your lips (Colossians 3:8 NIV).

My dear brothers and sisters, understand this: Everyone should be quick to listen, slow to speak, and slow to anger, for human anger does not accomplish God's righteousness (James 1:19-20 CSB).

DON'T GET DRUNK

It is important to note that the following verses do not say "don't drink." They say don't get drunk. That's an important difference. Good thing. Many people drink alcohol. According to the National Institute of Alcohol Abused and Alcoholism, over eighty five percent of adult Americans "reported that they drank alcohol at some point in their lifetime; 70.0 percent reported that they drank in the past year; and 55.3 percent reported that they drank in the past month."[91]

Thankfully, far fewer drink to drunkenness. The NIAAA reports that about twenty-five percent of American adults "engaged in binge drinking" in the preceding month, almost seven percent reported that they "engaged in heavy alcohol use" the preceding month.[92] Christians should not be among them.

Disciples:

Now the works of the flesh are obvious:...drunkenness, carousing... I am warning you about these things—as I warned you before—that those who practice such things will not inherit the kingdom of God (Galatians 5:19-21 CSB).

And don't get drunk with wine, which leads to reckless living, but be filled by the Spirit (Ephesians 5:18 CSB).

Don't Practice Idolatry

Dictionary.com defines idolatry as "the worship of idols; extreme admiration, love, or reverence for something or someone." Merriam-Webster defines it as "the worship of a physical object as a god; immoderate attachment or devotion to something." In times past, it was apparently very easy to end up worshiping idols.

Moses led the Jews out of 400 years of slavery in Egypt, the successful result of a series of miracles and plagues God himself used to soften Pharaoh's heart and demonstrate God's power. During their journey out of Egypt, Moses was on a mountain for forty days so God could personally hand him the Ten Commandments (the first two of which are to have no other gods before me and don't make any carved images). Even after all that God just did for them, what did many of the Jews do during those few days? They melted down a bunch of gold and made themselves a golden calf to worship. God was so mad he considered destroying them, but Moses talked him out of it. (Exodus 32.)

You would think they would have known better, having just been through what they'd been through and seen what they'd seen. Come on, people.

But are we any better? While it is easier to avoid worshiping a golden calf these days, we sure do worship people and physical objects, and become immoderately attached or devoted to our things, pretty readily. Think about how much importance we place on our things: our cars, houses, jewelry, and other signs of status. Think about how preoccupied we are with the words, deeds, wardrobes, and lifestyle of our "idols:" celebrities, politicians, and pundits. How much time do you spend informing yourself about God compared to informing yourself about them?

Disciples:

Do not be idolaters, as some of them were; as it is written: "The people sat down to eat and drink and got up to indulge in pagan revelry" (1 Corinthians 10:7 NIV).

So then, my dear friends, flee from idolatry (1 Corinthians 10:14 CSB).

Now the works of the flesh are obvious:... idolatry... I am warning you about these things—as I warned you before—that those who practice such things will not inherit the kingdom of God (Galatians 5:19-21 CSB).

For of this you can be sure: No immoral, impure or greedy person—such a man is an idolater—has any inheritance in the kingdom of Christ and of God (Ephesians 5:5 NIV).

Therefore, put to death what belongs to your earthly nature: sexual immorality, impurity, lust, evil desire, and greed, which is idolatry. Because of these, God's wrath is coming upon the disobedient, and you once walked in these things when you were living in them (Colossians 3:5-7 CSB).

Now you know the details of how Christians are supposed to conduct themselves. You also know how you actually conduct yourself. Ready to compare the two? The next chapter makes it easy to do so.

19

Take the Test

Test yourselves to see if you are in the faith. Examine yourselves.
Or do you yourselves not recognize that Jesus Christ is in you?—
Unless you fail the test (2 Corinthians 13:5 CSB).

This chapter suggests an analytical framework you can use to test yourself. I call it a test, for the sake of convenience, but it's really just one way of turning everything you have read into a set of standards against which you may measure yourself. There are other ways. If you have a better way, do it your way.

If you do take the test, you will see that the questions in Parts A and B are pass-fail, in keeping with the verses that do, or may, make these "thumbs up" or "thumbs down" issues. The questions in Parts C and D recognize that our behavior exists on a continuum; there is no clear "passing score" for any one of the listed behaviors in particular, much less all of them taken together. This being an intensely personal process that requires you to come to your own conclusions about such things, I leave it to you to decide what a passing score is and whether you pass. Now that you have a command of all of these verses and know yourself best, who would be better suited than you to do that?

At the risk of stating the obvious: this is not a one-time thing. However you do on the test today, you can score much higher (or lower) next month or next year depending on what you do with what you've learned. So, take the test periodically. Just remember that, while life appears to be a marathon and not a sprint, you don't actually know how long a race you are running or when you will finish.

Part A

Respond to the following statements, which cover the things the Bible teaches us are (or may be) essential to salvation:

1. I believe and have faith that Jesus was God's son.

    Yes_____   No_____   Don't Know_____

2. I believe and have faith that Jesus was crucified and rose from the dead.

    Yes_____   No_____   Don't Know_____

3. I believe and have faith that Jesus died on the cross as a sacrifice for the forgiveness of my sins, to save me from my sins and afford me eternal life.

    Yes_____   No_____   Don't Know_____

4. I accept Jesus as my Lord and Savior.

    Yes_____   No_____   Don't Know_____

5. The Holy Spirit dwells within me.

    Yes_____   No_____   Don't Know_____

6. If I have to repent of my sinful behavior to be a Christian, I have.

    Yes_____   No_____   Don't Know_____

7. If I have to forgive others for the wrongs they have committed against me to be a Christian, I have.

    Yes_____   No_____   Don't Know_____

8. If I have to be among the Elect to be a Christian, I am.

    Yes_____   No_____   Don't Know_____

If you answered all of these questions "Yes," you pass this part of the test. If you answered any of these questions "No," according to certain Bible verses, you fail the test. If you answered any of these questions "Don't Know," you need to be sure before you can be confident you pass the test.

Part B

Respond to the following statements, which cover the things the Bible teaches us prevent (or may prevent) a person from being saved:

1. I have fallen away from the Christian faith.
    Yes____   No____   Don't Know____
2   I have blasphemed against the Holy Spirit
    Yes____   No____   Don't Know____
3. I have denied Jesus before others.
    Yes____   No____   Don't Know____

If you answered all of these questions "No," you pass this part of the test. If you answered any of these questions "Yes," according to certain Bible verses, you fail the test. If you answered any of these questions "Don't Know," you need to be sure before you can be confident you pass the test.

Part C

Score yourself 0 to 10 on how well you do the following things that Christians are supposed to do. Total Available Points: 230. What you believe is a passing score:_____

Behavior	Score
1. My big picture looks like God's big picture.	____
2. I love and serve God.	____
3. I love others as I love myself.	____
4. I follow the Golden Rule.	____
5. I am holy.	____
6. I emulate the Beatitudes.	____
7. I am humble.	____
8. I serve others.	____
9. I am merciful.	____
10. I am charitable.	____
11. I am quietly compassionate and generous.	____
12. I forgive others.	____
13. I am introspective.	____
14. I use my gifts to further God's work.	____
15. I exercise good self-control.	____
16. I choose my words carefully.	____
17. I keep my word.	____

18. I treat my family well.   _____
19. I turn the other cheek.   _____
20. I pray.   _____
21. I acknowledge Christ.   _____
22. I obey those in authority.   _____
23. I gratefully rejoice.   _____
     Your Score   _____

Part D

Score yourself 0 to 10 on how well you refrain from doing the following things that Christians are not supposed to do. Total Available Points: 90. What you believe is a passing score:_____

Behavior	**Score**
1. I don't judge others.	_____
2. I don't worry, in general.	_____
3. I don't worry about money, in particular.	_____
4. I don't lie.	_____
5. I don't engage in sexually immoral behavior.	_____
6. I don't steal.	_____
7. I don't get angry.	_____
8. I don't get drunk.	_____
9. I don't practice idolatry.	_____
Your score:	_____

Final Grade

Result of Part A: Pass _____ or Fail _____
Result of Part B: Pass _____ or Fail _____
Result of Part C: Pass _____ or Fail _____
Result of Part D: Pass _____ or Fail _____

Final Result: Pass _____ or Fail _____

20

Suggestions

So, how did you do? If you are confident you are a Christian, fantastic. If you have concerns or doubts, join the club. Then do something about it. Remember: Where you find yourself today isn't the end of your Christian story. It's the beginning of the rest of that story. How the rest of your Christian story is written, and how it ends, is up to you and God.

How can those of us with doubts ever hope to conform our behavior to the high standards Jesus sets for us? We are not alone in having this question and concern: Jesus' disciples had exactly the same reaction to Jesus' statement that it is easier for a camel to go through the eye of a needle than for a rich person to enter the kingdom of God. They were "utterly astonished," and asked him, "Then who can be saved?" Jesus answered, "With man this is impossible, but with God all things are possible" (Matthew 19:24-26 CSB).

And, of course, Jesus himself acknowledged how difficult it is to live a Christian life.

"Enter through the narrow gate. For wide is the gate and broad is the road that leads to destruction, and many enter through it. But small is the gate and narrow the road that leads to life, and only a few find it" (Matthew 7:13 NIV).

"Lord," someone asked him, "are only a few people going to be saved?" He said to them, "Make every effort to enter through the narrow door, because I tell you many will try to enter and won't be able once the homeowner gets up and shuts the door. Then you will stand outside and knock on the door saying, 'Lord, open up for us!' He will answer you, 'I don't know you or where you're from.' Then you will say, 'We ate and drank in your presence, and you taught in our streets.' But he will say, 'I tell you, I don't know

you or where you're from. Get away from me, all you evil-doers!'" (Luke 13:23-27 CSB).

The jumping off point for living life in keeping with God's expectations is to recognize that you can't do it alone, but with God's help you can. How you and God accomplish that in your own life is entirely up to you and him, but I have ten suggestions that I hope will help the cause.

1. Be Deliberate

Don't walk around bumping into things, hoping your conduct matches up with God's expectations. As you decide to do or not do something, consider whether your intended actions are consistent with your obligations as a Christian. Think of your life as a journey toward an evermore Christ-like life.

2. Think of Your Actions as Acts of Worship

Regard each of your actions as an undertaking to glorify God. If your goal at the grocery store is to get out of there as quickly as possible, you will conduct yourself much differently than you will if your goal is to glorify God and pick up a few groceries while you are doing so. If your goal in a discussion with someone you disagree with is to glorify God, you will have that discussion much differently than if your goal is to win an argument.

3. Put Your Possessions in God's Service

There is nothing wrong with Christians having possessions, but there is tension between your obligations as a Christian and accumulating possessions for their own sake, out of selfishness, pride, or other worldly motivations. If you consider your possessions to be assets for serving God, however, it is easy to harmonize owning them with living a Christian life. Viewing your possessions through this lens, and acting accordingly, will turn your possessions from a source of concern into a source of comfort with respect to how well you are doing as a Christian.

4. Keep Good Company

Spend time with people who behave the way you would like to behave. It is much easier to be on good behavior when those around you are well behaved. It is much more difficult when those around you are tempting you to engage in behavior you are trying to avoid.

5. Avoid Temptation

Similarly, avoid circumstances that will tempt you to misbehave. If your weakness is a temptation to cheat on your spouse, it's a lot easier to avoid cheating while on a business trip if you are reading in your hotel room than if you are having a drink in the lobby bar with your wedding ring off. Remember James' promise: the devil will flee from you if you resist him (James 4:7). And remember this:

> *No temptation has overtaken you except what is common to mankind. And God is faithful; he will not let you be tempted beyond what you can bear. But when you are tempted, he will also provide a way out so that you can endure it* (1 Corinthians 10:13 NIV).

6. Read for Inspiration and Encouragement

Read books that inspire virtue and good behavior (in addition to the Bible, of course). *The Book of Virtues* and *The Moral Compass* by William Bennett are great places to start. Having examples to model your behavior after makes it easier to decide how to conduct yourself when you want to do the right thing but don't necessarily know what that is.

7. Attend Church

Attending church and church-related fellowship will put you in the company of like-minded people, many of whom are struggling with the same things you are. The messages you hear each Sunday should replenish your spiritual well and help keep you in the right track. (If they don't, consider finding another church.)

8. Use Reminders

Use the test in this book, or better still a list of your own creation, to remind yourself of the things that you are supposed to be doing, and not doing, as a Christian. Hang it on the refrigerator or keep it in your phone.

9. Start Small

If you have a long list of things you need to work on as a Christian, fixing all of them may seem like such an overwhelming undertaking that you don't know where to start—and so you may not start at all. Don't let that happen. Start somewhere. Prioritize the things you want to be better about and get going on the first one. When you feel good about that one, turn to the next one. You will get on a roll and find yourself where you want to be before you know it.

10. Pray

Jesus said that it is not possible to do this on your own. Don't try. Pray. Ask God for the help Jesus promised God would give you to live up to his expectations. Then, take a deep breath, do the best you can, and be on the lookout for his help. You will find it.

I hope these suggestions help. Whatever you do, don't respond to doubts about your faith with fear or resignation. Respond with action and enthusiastic commitment. Your life could have unfolded such that you only learned about Christ today. Act as if you did: pursue Christ as if you just met. You have time to bring yourself to a place of confidence in your faith; you just don't know how much. Use whatever time you have left wisely. Speaking of which, the next (and last) chapter explores the interesting, if academic, question of when Christians go to heaven and non-believers to hell.

21

When Do Christians Go to Heaven?

I have fought the good fight, I have finished the race, I have kept the faith. Now there is in store for me the crown of righteousness, which the Lord, the righteous Judge, will award to me on that day—and not only to me, but also to all who have longed for his appearing (2 Timothy 4:7-8 NIV).

I hope you feel good about your status as a Christian now (or, if you have concerns, after you speak with a member of the clergy) and confidently look forward to going to heaven. Even so, if you are like most people, you want to go—but not yet. Not yet.

Regardless of when we want to go to heaven, when will we actually go there? Does your soul go to heaven (and the souls of the unsaved to hell) immediately when you die, or does your soul sleep until the Rapture? The answer is academic, obviously, because Christians will enter heaven in God's good time. (Picture soul tapping foot, looking at watch and thinking, "Come on already!")

Still, the question is interesting. It is even more interesting because—you guessed it—different verses support different conclusions. Some verses suggest that the souls of some people immediately arrived at their ultimate destination after death. For example, in the conversation between Jesus and the repentant criminal on the cross beside him, which we covered earlier:

Then he said, "Jesus, remember me when you come into your kingdom." And he said to him, "Truly I tell you, today you will be with me in paradise" (Luke 23:43 CSB).

Perhaps this person received special treatment given the circumstances. If applicable to all of us, however, Jesus' words indicate that Christians arrive in paradise upon their deaths.

Elijah, who most certainly received special treatment, was taken to heaven before he even died (2 Kings 2:11). Moses did not receive such treatment; he died and was buried in a grave (Deuteronomy 34:5-6). Nevertheless, many years later, the disciples saw Moses and Elijah with Jesus during the Transfiguration (Matthew 17:1-4). These verses suggest that, like the repentant criminal on the cross, Moses and Elijah went to heaven directly after their time on earth was finished, rather than to sleep to await the Second Coming.

Jesus' story of the Rich Man and Lazarus suggests the same. In that story, Jesus described people going straight to heaven and hell, respectively, immediately upon their deaths.

"The time came when the beggar died and the angels carried into Abraham's side. The rich man also died and was buried. In Hades, where he was in torment, he looked up and saw Abraham far away, with Lazarus by his side" (Luke 16:22-23 NIV).

Assuming Abraham was in heaven (a safe assumption, I hope), in this story Jesus said that angels took Lazarus directly to heaven when he died. The rich man went immediately to hell. It is clear that both ended up in their ultimate destinations before Judgement Day, because the rich man asked Abraham to send Lazarus to warn his brothers (who were still living in their father's house) of the torment that awaits non-believers (Luke 16:27).

The following verses from the book of Revelation describe souls of the dead coming out of the sea, out of death, and out of Hades on Judgment Day. Presumably, they went there when they died:

Then I saw a great white throne and one seated on it. Earth and heaven fled from his presence and no place was found for them. I also saw the dead, the great and the small, standing before the throne, and books were opened. Another book was opened, which is the book of life, and the dead were judged according to their works by what was written in the books. Then the sea gave up the dead that were in it, and death and Hades gave up the dead that were in them; each one was judged according to their works. Death and Hades were thrown into the lake of fire. This is the second death, the lake of fire. And anyone whose name was not found written in the book of life was thrown into the lake of fire (Revelation 20:11-15 CSB).

So, a number of verses give us reason to believe that Christians go straight to heaven, and nonbelievers straight to hell, when they die. But if that's the case, what will happen at Jesus' Rapture—when the dead in Christ are resurrected?

The prophet Daniel foretold the resurrection of the souls of the dead at the Rapture, both the souls of those who will be saved and the souls of those who will not. Recounting what God said to him, Daniel wrote:

At that time Michael, the great prince who stands watch over your people, will rise up. There will be a time of distress such as never has occurred since nations came into being until that time. But at that time all your people who are found written in the book will escape. Many who sleep in the dust of the earth will awake, some to eternal life, and some to disgrace and eternal contempt (Daniel 12:1-2 CSB).

It is interesting that Daniel reports that "many who sleep in the dust of the earth," not "all who sleep in the dust of the earth," will awake. Who are the people that will not, why will they not awake, and what will happen to them? We will have to wait and see.

Those questions aside, for our purposes it is clear that some of those who sleep in the dust of the earth will awake to eternal life, meaning that they are Christians. Others who sleep in the dust will awake to eternal contempt, meaning that they are not. But, according to these verses, neither Christians nor non-Christians go immediately to their ultimate destinations when they die, but instead will "sleep in the dust" until the Second Coming. In fact, Jesus said that no one but him has entered heaven:

"No one has ever gone into heaven except the one who came from heaven—the Son of Man" (John 3:13 NIV).

I will leave it to you to reconcile this verse with the Old Testament account of Elijah. But, in keeping with this verse and Daniel's prophecy, many verses in the New Testament speak of a resurrection. They imply or expressly state that those who will be resurrected are in their graves, or somewhere else, from which they will be "raised up." These verses say this of both Christians and non-Christians.

Jesus:

"On the contrary, when you host a banquet, invite those who are poor, maimed, lame, or blind. And you will be blessed, because they cannot repay you; for you will be repaid at the resurrection of the righteous" (Luke 14:13-14 CSB).

"Do not be amazed at this, for a time is coming when all who are in their graves will hear his voice and come out—those who have done what is good will rise to live, and those who have done what is evil will rise to be condemned" (John 5:28-29 NIV).

"This is the will of him who sent me: that I should lose none of these he has given me but should raise them up on the last day. For this is the will of my Father: that everyone who sees the Son and believes in him will have eternal life, and I will raise him up on the last day" (John 6:39-40 CSB).

"No one can come to me unless the Father who sent me draws them, and I will raise them up at the last day" (John 6:44 NIV).

Disciples:

I have a hope in God, which these men themselves also accept, that there will be a resurrection, both of the righteous and the unrighteous (Acts 24:15 CSB).

Now if Christ is proclaimed as raised from the dead, how can some of you say, "There is no resurrection of the dead"? If there is no resurrection of the dead, then not even Christ has been raised; and if Christ has not been raised, then our proclamation is in vain, and so is your faith. Moreover, we are found to be false witnesses about God, because we have testified wrongly about God that he raised up Christ—whom he did not raise up, if in fact the dead are not raised. For if the dead are not raised, not even Christ has been raised. And if Christ has not been raised, your faith is worthless; you are still in your sins. Those, then, who have fallen asleep in Christ have also perished. If we have put our hope in Christ for this life only, we should be pitied more than anyone (1 Corinthians 15:12-19 CSB).

But in fact Christ has been raised from the dead, the first fruits of those who have died. For since death came through a human being, the resurrection of the dead has also come through a human being; for as all die in Adam, so all will be made alive in Christ. But each in his own order: Christ the first fruits, then at his coming those who belong to Christ. Then comes the end, when he hands over the kingdom to God the Father, after he has destroyed every ruler and every authority and power (1 Corinthians 15:20-24 NRSV).

But someone will ask, "How are the dead raised? What kind of body will they have when they come?" You fool! What you sow does not come to life unless it dies. And as for what you sow— you are not sowing the body that will be, but only the seed, perhaps of wheat or another grain. But God gives it a body as he wants, and to each of the seeds its own body. Not all flesh is the same flesh; there is one was for humans, another for animals, another for birds, and another for fish. There are heavenly bodies and earthly bodies, but the splendor of the heavenly bodies is different from that of the earthly ones. There is a splendor of the sun, another of the moon, and another of the stars; in fact, one star differs from another star in splendor. So it is with the resurrection of the dead: sown in corruption, raised in incorruption; sown in dishonor, raised in glory; sown in weakness, raised in power; sown a natural body, raised a spiritual body (1 Corinthians 15:35-44 CSB).

The first man was of the dust of the earth; the second man is of heaven. As was the earthly man, so are those who are of the earth; and as is the heavenly man, so also are those who are of heaven. And just as we have borne the image of the earthly man, so shall we bear the image of the heavenly man (1 Corinthians 15:47-49 NIV).

What I am saying, brothers and sisters, is this: Flesh and blood cannot inherit the kingdom of God, nor can corruption inherent incorruption. Listen, I am telling you a mystery: We will not all fall asleep, but we will all be changed, in a moment, in the twinkling of an eye, at the last trumpet. For the trumpet will sound, and the dead will be raised incorruptible, and we will be changed (1 Corinthians 15:50-52 CSB).

Brothers and sisters, we do not want you to be uninformed about those who sleep in death, so that you do not grieve like the rest of mankind, who have no hope. For we believe that Jesus died and rose again, and so we believe that God will bring with Jesus those who have fallen asleep in him. According to the Lord's word, we tell you that we who are still alive, who are left until the coming of the Lord, will certainly not precede those who have fallen asleep. For the Lord himself will come down from heaven, with a loud command, with the voice of the archangel and with the trumpet call of God, and the dead in Christ will rise first. After that, we who are still alive and are left will be caught up together with them in the clouds to meet the Lord in the air. And so we will be with the Lord forever (1 Thessalonians 4:13-17 NIV).

When Christ, who is your life, appears, then you also will appear with him in glory (Colossians 3:4 CSB).

I saw thrones on which were seated those who had been given authority to judge. And I saw the souls of those who had been beheaded because of their testimony about Jesus and because of the word of God. They had not worshiped the beast or its image and had not received its mark on their foreheads or their hands. They came to life and reigned with Christ a thousand years. (The rest of the dead did not come to life until the thousand years were ended.) This is the first resurrection (Revelation 20:4-5 NIV).

Regardless of when we get to heaven, I hope reading this book helps you find—and if you are already on it, stay on—the path that leads there. If you are new to the faith, that path may start with exploring your relationship with Christ. If you are a long-time believer, this segment of that path may involve renewing, expanding, and deepening your relationship with him. Wherever you are on your spiritual journey, I pray that, when that journey ends, this book will help you be one taken.

Endnotes

1 www.foxnews.com, "Christian singer makes shocking announcement: 'I no longer believe in God,'" visited May 26, 2020.

2 www.pewresearch.org, "Key findings about Americans' belief in God," visited May 23, 2020.

3 www.news.gallup.com, "In Depth: Topics A to Z: Religion", visited May 23, 2020.

4 Id.

5 www.news.gallup.com, "Politics: U.S. Church Membership Down Sharply in Past Two Decades," visited May 23, 2020.

6 Id.

7 www.nrm.org, "Golden Rule," visited May 10, 2020.

8 Wikipedia, "Golden Rule," visited May 10, 2020.

9 www.thepastorsworkshop.com, "Sermon Quotes, The Beatitudes," quoting Dallas Willard, "The Divine Conspiracy," visited May 24, 2020.

10 www.psychologicalscience.org, "Measuring Humility and Its Positive Effects," visited May 24, 2020.

11 www.ncbi.nlm.nih.gov, "Evidence for arrogance: On the relative importance of expertise, outcome, and manner," visited May 24, 2020.

12 Id.

13 www.mentalfloss.com, "7 Scientific Benefits of Helping Others," visited May 24, 2020.

14 Id.

15 www.abcnews.go.com, "Amish School Shooter's Widow, Marie Monville, Speaks Out," visited June 7, 2020.

16 Id.

17 Id.

18 www.charitychoices.com; "How much is given? By Whom? For what?", visited June 7, 2020.

19 Id.

20 Id.

21 Id.

22 www.nonprofitssource.com, "Church And Religious Charitable Giving Statistics," visited June 7, 2020.

23 Id.

[24] www.cdfcapital.org, "Significant Statistics about Tithing and Church Generosity," visited June 7, 2020.

[25] Id.

[26] Id.

[27] www.dailymail.co.uk, "Woman shows incredible mercy as her son's killer moves in next door," visited May 24, 2020.

[28] Id.

[29] Id.

[30] www.forbes.com, "Only 15% of People are Self-Aware—Here's How to Change," visited May 25, 2020.

[31] Id.

[32] www.britannica.com, "Albert Einstein, German-American Physicist," visited May 25, 2020.

[33] www.nytimes.com, "Billy Graham, 99, Dies; Pastor Filled Stadiums and Counseled Presidents," visited May 25, 2020.

[34] Id.

[35] www.reflectd.co, "8 Scientific Facts about Self-Control," visited May 25, 2020.

[36] Id.

[37] www.happierhuman.com, "Self Control," visited May 25, 2020.

[38] www.entrepreneur.com, "The Importance of Cultivating Self-Discipline," visited May 25, 2020.

[39] www.time.com, "The Divorce Rate is Dropping. That May Not Actually Be Good News," visited May 25, 2020.

[40] www.fatherhood.org, "Father Absence + Involvement Statistics," visited May 25, 2020.

[41] www.christianpost.com, "'42' the Jackie Robinson Story: Turning the Other Cheek," visited June 7, 2020.

[42] Id.

[43] www.pewforum.org, "Religious Landscape Study, Frequency of Prayer," visited June 8, 2020.

[44] Id.

[45] www.barna.com, "Silent and Solo: How Americans Pray," visited June 8, 2020.

[46] Id.

[47] Id.

48 Id.

49 Id.

50 www.bbc.com, "Christian persecution 'at near genocide levels'," visited June 8, 2020.

51 Id.

52 Id.

53 www.statista.com, "Number of anti-religion hate crime incidents in the United States in 2018, by religion," visited June 8, 2020.

54 www.nypost.com, "Protestors burn Bible, American flag as tensions rise in Portland," visited August 4, 2020.

55 www.nytimes.com, "Church That Defied Coronavirus Restrictions Is Burned to Ground," visited August 4, 2020; www.usnews.com, "Mississippi Church Suing on Virus Restrictions Burns Down," visited August 4, 2020.

56 www.denisonforum.org, "Churches burned across the country: Why was this not national news?," visited August 3, 2020.

57 www.time.com," Regular Christians Are No Longer Welcome in American Culture," visited June 8, 2020.

58 C.S. Lewis, "Reflections on the Psalms."

59 www.adaa.org, "Facts & Statistics," visited May 27, 2020.

60 www.webmd.com, "Physical Effects of Worrying" visited May 27, 2020.

61 www.huffpost.com, "85 Percent of What We Worry About Never Happens," visited May 27, 2020.

62 Id.

63 www.cnbc.com, "Americans are more stressed about money than work or relationships – here's why," visited May 27, 2020.

64 Id.

65 www.cnbc.com, "25% of Americans say they worry about money 'all the time'," visited May 27, 2020.

66 www.apa.org, "Money stress weighs on Americans' health," visited May 27, 2020.

67 Id.

68 www.ted.com, "The truth about lying," visited May 16, 2020.

69 www.newscientist.com, "Lies, damned lies, and here are the statistics," visited May 16, 2020.

70 www.umass.edu, "UMass Amherst Researcher Finds Most People Lie in

Everyday Conversation," visited May 23, 2020.

[71] www.msu.edu, "The Prevalence of Lying in America: Three Studies of Self-Reported Lies," visited May 23, 2020.

[72] www.yaleglobal.yale.edu, "World Agrees: Adultery, While Prevalent, Is Wrong," visited May 23, 2020.

[73] Id.

[74] Id.

[75] Id.

[76] Id.

[77] Id..

[78] www.foxbusiness.com, "Coronavirus mandates lead to Ashley Madison membership surge," visited May 16, 2020.

[79] www.thehollywoodgossip.com, "23 Celebrity Virgins: Who's Waiting (or Waited) Until Marriage?", visited May 27, 2020.

[80] www.people.com; "Celebrities Reveal the Number of People They've Slept with – and the Numbers Go as High as 20,000," visited May 27, 2020.

[81] Id.

[82] www.npr.org, "A Couple Opens Up About Their Decision to Wait Until Marriage Before Having Sex," visited May 27, 2020.

[83] www.waitingtillmarriage.org, "4 Cool Statistics About Abstinence in the USA," visited May 27, 2020.

[84] www.britannica.com, "Bernie Madoff, American Hedge-Fund Investor," visited May 27, 2020.

[85] www.ucr.fbi.gov, "2018 Crime in the United States, Larceny-Theft," visited May 27, 2020.

[86] Id.

[87] www.shiftprocessing.com, "Credit Card Fraud Statistics," visited May 27, 2020.

[88] Id.

[89] www.angermanage.co.uk, "Anger Statistics," visited May 16, 2020.

[90] Id.

[91] www.niaaa.nih.gov, "Alcohol Facts and Statistics," visited May 16, 2020.

[92] Id.

About the Author

BRETT PRESTON majored in Religion at Duke University, attended law school at Washington University in St. Louis, and has practiced law since 1986. A "lawyer's lawyer," Brett represents lawyers in legal malpractice cases, and Best Lawyers has three times named him "Lawyer of the Year" for his work in that field in the Tampa Bay area. He also represents corporate clients in a wide variety of complex lawsuits. He and his wife live in Tampa, and they have three adult children.

The author would welcome your comments, questions, or other communications about *One Taken* through his email at OneTaken@mail.com or his cell, 813.504.6745.

CPSIA information can be obtained
at www.ICGtesting.com
Printed in the USA
BVHW040958250621
610376BV00007B/1547